Extreme Spirituality

Radical Approaches
to Awakening

Tolly Burkan

COUNCIL OAK BOOKS
SAN FRANCISCO/TULSA

Council Oak Books, LLC

2105 E. 15th

Tulsa, OK 74104

©2001 by Firewalking Institute of Research and Education.

Originally published by Beyond Words Publishing, Inc

First Council Oak Books edition 2004

Printed in Canada

LIBRARY OF CONGRESS CATALOGING-IN-PUBLICATION DATA

Burkan, Tolly.
  Extreme spirituality : radical approaches to awakening / Tolly Burkan.
    p. cm.
  ISBN 1-57178-162-5
  1. Spiritual life. 2. Mortification. I. Title.
  BL625.B854 2004
  204'.47--dc22

                     2004016868

To Sandra Leicester, with gratitude
for her inspiration.

NOTE

There is an inherent risk in many of the practices described in this book. Readers are cautioned that it is always advisable to have an experienced instructor guide them through these spiritual practices, and to exercise common sense. The author and publisher are not responsible for injuries—mental, physical, or financial—that may result from a reader attempting any of the practices or exercises described in *Extreme Spirituality*.

CONTENTS

ACKNOWLEDGMENTS

I want to acknowledge Sandra Leicester not only for inspiring this book, but for her ongoing nurturing of the writing process ... creating the title and subtitle for the book ... and offering insightful feedback on everything from cover ideas to text revisions. I want to thank my parents Eileen and Ted Burkan for being the first to read the completed manuscript; I greatly appreciate their constructive suggestions. Despite an over-burdening pull at his time, my brother Barry then spent many generous hours editing the rough manuscript. Thank you Barry.

I'd like to acknowledge Richard Cohn and Cindy Black for their resolve to serve the multitudes and make a difference in the world, especially by publishing books such as this. Laura Carlsmith and Julie Steigerwaldt were not only uplifting women to have as editors, they made the book sparkle in a way that will touch more people. I want them both to know how much they are appreciated.

Andrew Weil gets my heartfelt gratitude for opening the eyes of so many individuals world-wide to the fact that they can take an active part in creating the lives they want. However, I want to primarily thank him for his contribution to this book. His foreword shares wisdom that everyone can understand. Thank you, Andrew.

FOREWORD
By Andrew Weil, M.D.

What is extreme spirituality? It is accepting, even embracing, challenging situations in order to grow in spirit. Firewalking can be an example of this. Many people wonder why anyone would voluntarily walk across red-hot coals. Well, as one who has firewalked a number of times, I can tell you that firewalking can be, like the other extreme spiritual practices you'll read about in this book, a powerful and potentially transformative act. Done with the right attitude and expectations, it strips away your self-imposed limits. It brings you to a clarity where you see the difference between your ego—your worry-based, me-centered self—and your divine nature.

As father of the firewalking movement, Tolly Burkan's main achievement is not simply his methods—anyone can burn wood and invite others to traverse hot coals. Tolly's genius is in demonstrating that firewalking is not foreign and unattainable. Like other extreme practices, it is simply a tool to help us see our self-created limitations, and is far from being freakish and esoteric. Tolly's message in this book is of excitement and hope: you can do anything you decide you want to.

Let me briefly summarize my experience of three firewalks. From my experiences—both good and not so good—you can see how your decisions and expectations can influence how you perceive obstacles.

In January 1984, Tolly Burkan came to my house outside Tucson to present a firewalking workshop. About eighty people attended, including twenty medical students from the University of Arizona. Tolly presented us with the information you are about to read, and then we filed out to a horse corral under a clear, starry desert sky. A huge bonfire had burned down to coals. Tolly raked the coals into a bed two feet wide and twelve feet long. It would take four steps to get from one end to the other.

The bed of coals felt very hot to everyone who approached it. The wood used was pinyon pine and pecan, a hot-burning combination. It was "one of the hottest" fires, in Tolly's words, and he had seen more firepits than anyone else. The group was in an expectant mood.

Tolly walked first, and I was one of the next to cross. I should describe my state of mind-body before I tell what happened to my feet. I was in good to average physical condition and had not done anything to toughen my feet. My emotional state was also average, but I felt mentally scattered. My parents were present at the firewalk, as was my boss from the college of medicine, who was quite concerned about the safety of the students. My dog had just had ten puppies, and they were crying in the upstairs bedroom. As the organizer of the firewalk, I felt responsible for the success of the evening and somewhat pressured to do the walk early and set a good example.

From the first step, the coals felt burning hot, which came as a great surprise. I was able to cross without faltering or registering pain, but the pain was near my limit. I do not think I could have taken more than one or two additional steps, and I was very happy to get onto the cold wet ground at the far end. While I was somewhat distracted before and during my walk, afterward I was aware of feeling altered: an adrenaline high plus exalted relief and a strong feeling of camaraderie with the other walkers. The soles of my feet burned and tingled, although I could not pay much attention to them because so much else was going on.

I watched others walk over the coals. From the way they moved, most, but not all, seemed to have the same experience I did. A few of those who walked that night said they had felt no sensation of heat. They also had no marks on their feet.

When the coals were doused, we all filed back into the house, still feeling elated. The sensations in my feet resolved into a few burning spots that hurt enough to keep me from sleeping soundly that night. By the next morning, the pain was mostly gone.

What I learned from that first try was that you can walk on fire in at least two different ways. First, it is not that hard just to tough out a twelve-foot walk by taking purposeful strides, maintaining a stoic attitude, and not doing anything foolish like stopping or falling in. The worst injury is likely to be some localized first- and second-degree burns of minor consequence. On a practical level, it is useful to know that if only to demystify firewalking and lend support to the idea that anyone can do it.

Alternatively, and more beneficially, you can walk in some other state of mind-body in which sensation and tissue responses are different from normal. Encouraging you to find that "altered state" where your mind, and even your body, are under your control, is what this book is all about. Knowing that I hadn't attained it with my first walk, I wanted to try again.

My next chance to firewalk came six months later, again at my house, but this time with a small group of twelve, only half of whom walked. The leader was a local tai ch'i teacher who, despite his lack of formal instruction, had decided he could teach firewalking. But he was not able to create any of the group feeling of personal power and joy that Tolly had been able to encourage in us participants.

On this occasion I was in top physical condition, having just returned from a ten-day program of fasting, prayers, cleansing, and exercise on the Big Island of Hawaii. I had been barefoot a lot, so the soles of my feet were tougher than usual. I was emotionally satisfied, filled with tropical beach energy, strong, and confident. Despite these positives, I felt no connection with the other people present, however; again, I felt internal pressure to do the walk and get it over with.

This was a shorter, cooler walk. The firepit was eight feet long, crossable in three steps. Despite the cooler coals, the sensation of burning heat was even more intense than before, so much so that I hopped through the last stride onto the safe ground beyond the far end of the coals. I knew I had burned my feet, and that thought detracted from any sense of accomplishment. In fact, as I soon found, I had a number of second-degree burns on both feet. They remained sore and interfered with walking for three weeks. Most of the others who walked that night also got burned.

No more firewalking for me, I decided. I was deflated and somewhat embarrassed that I was unable to master this art. Certainly I would never try it again unless I had reason to think it would be different.

So, when a friend invited me to another firewalk, I listened to him with a mixture of interest, excitement, and fear. All of these feelings intensified when he told me the group would be walking a firepit that was forty feet long.

The leader had learned firewalking from Tolly, and then developed his own style and techniques. The firewalk was the climactic event of a leadership training. By the time everyone went out to the fire, it was one in the morning, under a chilly, starry sky.

There were three firepits, neat, parallel, and red-hot. The wood was mesquite, which burns quite hot. The short walk was twelve feet. The others were forty feet, and looked awesomely long. I told myself I was just there to watch, but along with most other people, I found myself practicing the breathing and mental techniques being taught, and even getting into line at one of the forty-footers. I told myself I could cut out at the last moment, unless I got into some "different" state: otherwise I would be crazy to try it again.

This time I was in not-so-good physical and emotional condition. I had a lingering respiratory flu, giving me a sore throat and sore muscles. My feet were tender from not being out of shoes in a long while. I was depressed. It seemed unlikely that I could surmount these draining influences.

Nevertheless, I got caught up in the group excitement, which made me feel I was a member of a revival meeting or a celebrant of some tribal ritual. An ensemble of African drummers provided a rousing background tempo. Those huge beds of coals glowed incredibly in the night. People shouted and crowded toward them.

I was far forward in the line. As my turn approached, I felt a totally novel sensation: tingling energy rushing up my forearms from my hands. It was something like paresthesia (pins and needles) and something like electricity. At first I thought it might be an effect of hyperventilation, since I had been doing vigorous deep breathing, but the rest of my body did not feel hyperventilated, and in a few moments more, the sensations intensified and spread throughout my body. I took it as a sign of the altered state I was looking for, and suddenly knew that I could walk safely across forty feet of hot coals.

I did! There was no sensation of heat or burning, nor was I surprised at that. The coals just felt crunchy. When I got to the other end, forty short feet away, I was somewhere else for a few seconds, then came back to ordinary reality and realized what I'd done. I could have turned around, and walked all the way back to the beginning, too! I was certain of that. I felt strong, healthy, and incredibly high. This was what I had wanted to do. My previous two trips made this success even sweeter.

Through this extreme practice, I had achieved my goal of increasing my personal power: I had consciously controlled my attention and my thoughts, and through the excitement of the group, was encouraged to expect the best of myself and the situation.

Since then I have worked to re-create that state of power and enthusiasm. I practice by walking barefoot over a long (ninety feet) driveway paved with crushed rock. Unless I fully attend to the situation, I cannot take more than a few hesitant steps on the driveway. Only when I focus my attention and believe that I can overcome any obstacle, I reach the state of mind-body in which I can stride down its whole length without hurting my feet. That is the feeling I created in myself at the last firewalk. It is harder to get into without the group spirit, but it can be done.

The practices described in this book can help you get to this state. They'll help you recognize how incredibly powerful you are. The book distills all the challenges that life can throw your way into recognizable, albeit unusual, experiences. Either by reading about them, or actually doing them, you metaphorically address your fears. You see how possible it is to overcome your own limitations and how exhilarating it is to actually choose your own reality. Instead of pain, you choose power. Instead of anger, you choose forgiveness. Instead of judgment, you choose acceptance.

This book is a portal to a more spiritually oriented life. I urge you to accept Tolly's challenge to an extreme spirituality: a celebration of your best possibilities and a decision to create the most from any situation that you encounter. When you do, it's not only your mind that is altered: it's your body, too. When you achieve the desired state of consciousness, you can physiologically change your body's response to danger, tension and stress.

As unrelated as they may seem, extreme spirituality has profound implications for both health and medicine. It demonstrates the limitations of the model now dominant in the health sciences. A new model, in which consciousness is primary, not only makes more sense in relation to our own experiences of health, but also provides more options for positive human behavior. Such a model encourages us to recognize that we take an active part in shaping our responses to environmental stimuli, and that we need not be passive victims of them.

As with all the spiritual practices and exercises in this book, firewalking demonstrates how, through nonordinary states of consciousness, we can modify our body's responses to ordinarily harmful external stimulation. What does that mean? Well, if you don't have to experience pain, redness, and blisters on exposure to red-hot coals, then you don't have to get infections on exposure to germs, allergies on exposure to allergens, cancer on exposure to carcinogens. What a largely uncharted territory in which to discover powerful new techniques to bolster natural resistance to disease!

And what an exciting new paradigm with which to face suffering and challenges. Once you've walked on fire, once you've learned to love your enemies, once you've learned to break boards with your bare hands, you'll find the strength within to face any obstacle life places before you.

1
Introduction
What is Extreme Spirituality?

*Love lives in giving and forgiving. Ego lives
in getting and forgetting.*
–Sathya Sai Baba

We live in exciting times. Millions of people have walked on fire and haven't been burned. People are willing to learn how to break boards and bricks with their bare hands, sit in sweat lodges, skydive, shave their heads, and snap pointed arrows with their throats. Some of us experience spontaneous healing. What does this all mean? Are we getting closer to our true nature? Do these things give us a compass back to God? Are we proving that we create our own realities?

You are about to be challenged, shocked, and stimulated as you absorb the uncomplicated directives of the new spiritual paradigm described in *Extreme Spirituality*. Since 1973, when I was only twenty-five years old, I have been teaching people about inner growth. In my seminars, people find ways of tapping into their full potential. This book will take you on a journey that is similar to what people experience in my classes. You'll learn how to assume a totally spiritual perspective in every situation.

If you accept the truth that you create your own reality, then challenging situations can be experienced in one of two ways, either with stress or without stress. By assuming a spiritual perspective, any situation can either be enjoyed in some fashion or provide insight for spiritual growth. By choosing growth over suffering, a person demonstrates spiritual maturity.

Our spiritual selves are clothed in what has commonly come to be known as the ego. Most laypeople experience the ego as that part of themselves that makes them unique. It is the interface between what I call me, and not me. Most of us are so married to the activity of our egos, we believe they are who we actually are. At any given point, however, you can have an extreme experience that precipitates an awakening, an ego death, where you achieve the ability to watch your every activity, almost as though you were observing an actor on a movie screen. This omniscient watcher is who you really are. While the ego can think, feel, and be aware, the watcher, the larger you, is aware of everything that the small, ego-encompassed you is aware of.

If the everyday you is aware that you have a stomachache, the larger you can also be aware that the small you is aware of your stomach aching. If you are feeling exuberant over winning the lottery, you can watch yourself feeling the exuberance.

This ability to be aware that we are aware, i.e., to be conscious and create for ourselves an objective, detached way of observing our own lives, distinguishes us from every other animal on the planet. However, getting to this awareness is not a matter of a single decision. It requires a commitment to a process of ongoing spiritual growth, and it requires practice.

MANY BELIEVERS ARE BECOMING DOERS

To start your extreme journey of the spirit, as a conscious discipline try separating your awareness from your personality and daily activities. Practice being a witness to yourself: there I am talking, there I am laughing, there I am thinking, there I am reacting with anger, there I am experiencing love. Label the real you as the watcher of the movie. The person acting in your movie is your ego. Because most people are so identified with their egos, the process of letting go of it feels similar to death . . . because what dies is everything you have ever identified with being yourself.

Spiritual growth is a gradual transition from identifying with the ego-self into a realization and recognition of what is ego and what is conscious awareness. The Me Generation of the seventies was frequently ridiculed as being self-obsessed because ego was so preoccupied with itself. You need to be cautious that the little you doesn't keep thinking that it is the larger you. The way to tell the difference is simple: the little you will have judgments about itself. However, the larger conscious awareness witnesses without any judgment. It never says, "Whoops, you blew it again, you dummy." Rather, it just notices what is going on.

Allowing your ego to die may seem like an incongruous way to experience life, but the opposite is true. When you are not reacting, but instead are the cause of your life, making conscious choices and decisions, there is more and more joy to savor. It is a joy to watch your life unfold, just as you might enjoy a good novel, page after page, or a movie, as a parent enjoys watching videotapes of the children growing up.

This willingness to die is a desired state of being. The Hindu *Upanishads* speak of this ego-death as a state where you finally identify with the timelessness that resides within you. *This* never dies. Buddhism,

Taoism, and other Eastern religions, which account for two-thirds of the world's population, maintain that who we really are, our spiritual essence, can never die. But this realization only comes when you are willing to let the ego-self die. You see your true self as eternal.

At one holy temple in Sri Lanka, before you can enter, you must smash a coconut on a large stone standing by the temple door. The coconut represents your head. The ritual symbolizes your willingness to die for God. It is a profound spiritual experience to see your true self as something apart from your ego and body.

This metaphorical surrendering of the ego, of accepting death at the temple gate, would seem like a sacrifice, but it is simply relinquishing smallness, pettiness, and the mundane for bliss. Orgasm is often called a *petit mort,* or "little death," because there is a moment of bliss at the point where there's no experiencer, no ego, just pure beingness. Though it is fleeting, this "death" gives so much energy that the physical effort required to attain orgasm can hardly be termed a chore. There is an investment of energy in one form, and a reaping of even greater energy in another form.

LEAVING THE JUNGLE BEHIND

Ego originally served humans as part of the fight or flight mechanism that perpetuates our species. It was the impetus for self-preservation. This jungle mechanism is no longer a productive technique for survival. Physical self-preservation, for most of us in developed countries, is no longer an issue. Now, to survive as a species, we need to find ways to cooperate. We must learn to use the ego to go beyond the ego, to see life with a higher consciousness. Most of us cannot imagine there is any other way of experiencing reality than the way we have experienced it before. We cannot conceive of being set free from the known and familiar universe that we believe to be the only universe.

To complicate the matter, individual egos create different universes for each person. So we never can be sure of knowing what someone else's reality is. The universe of your neighbor, or even your spouse, is totally different from the universe you experience in your daily life. No wonder our society is filled with loneliness and anxiety. Because we cannot imagine other people's realities, we feel separate from them, isolated and alone.

That's why the time has come for a new spirituality, an extreme spirituality. And this process of dissociating from the ego is its entry point, whether it's a near-death experience, a mystical experience, grace, a shock, or one of the practices in this book.

EVOLUTION PROMPTS ADAPTATION

As human beings, we are not supposed to remain static. In fact, the only thing constant is the certainty of change. Our cells die and regenerate continually, so our physical bodies change. Every seven years we evolve into new phases of growth, so emotionally we change. Think of yourself at seven years old, then again at age fourteen, then at twenty-one, twenty-eight, and thirty-five. Weren't you a completely different person every seven years? Weren't you dealing with different issues and challenges at each of these ages than the ones facing you seven years earlier? Change is certain. People with personal power control how they change and choose who they become as a result of it. Without personal power, you can never really feel in control of your life, and you often feel like the victim of change.

The ability to create personal power is not genetic. It is a skill. What's surprising is how simple it is to master. Simple doesn't necessarily mean easy. It isn't easy to learn how to ride a two-wheeler. But it isn't that difficult. And once you've mastered it, you have that skill for a lifetime. It's the same with personal power.

SPIRITUAL GROWTH AS AN EXTREME SPORT

This book can help take you to the place that Buddha called the "end of suffering," otherwise known as enlightenment or nirvana. The end of suffering means you no longer react emotionally to situations by automatically responding with anger, hate, jealousy, depression, or any other negative emotion. Being in this state is EXTREME SPIRITUALITY in capital letters! And it will help you find or strengthen your personal power.

There are many ways to attain this enlightenment. *Extreme Spirituality* can help you on your journey by showing you how to adopt a spiritual perspective in any situation, which enables you to maintain your happiness and equilibrium. Once you have learned not to react, but to choose your reality, you can see a spiritual perspective in seemingly horrific situations that used to make you suffer. You will have found your power. Even when disaster befalls you, you'll no longer react with negative and uncomfortable emotions, but will see a larger picture, one in which the universe is perfect and everything in it is an aspect of divine order. You can actually *re-create* the universe in which you live. You have that power!

Extreme spirituality is any experience you can use to demonstrate to yourself how your ego masks, limits, distorts, or in any way diminishes your knowledge of a greater reality, and keeps you from finding your own personal power. It is any practice that enhances your experience of love, wisdom, and compassion, revealing aspects of your divine nature and leaving you with a crystal clear distinction between how your ego and your higher-self function.

This book describes exercises and practices I've used to get people into this mode of living with conscious awareness. If you can receive value from reading about these spiritual practices, great! You may wish to do some of them yourself. Anything you can use to get yourself into the mode of nonreaction will assist you in creating your own reality, one that no longer includes suffering of any kind. It is, simply put, the end of suffering.

I will end with a parable:

> *In medieval Japan, a youth claimed he longed for nothing but God, so he sought a Zen Master for guidance. The Master took the lad to a water barrel and abruptly forced the boy's head under water. When the young man lapsed into unconsciousness, the Master removed his head from the water and laid his limp body on the ground. After the boy revived, the Master said, "When you want God as much as you wanted air, you will have God."*

Do you want God *that* much? Do you want the power to create your own reality and live the life that you deserve? This new millennium is about realizing your true potential. It is the logical next step for humans as a species. Inner growth is the new frontier. It is extreme spirituality.

2
Firewalking
Pay Attention, Expect the Best, Go for It!

*I asked for strength, and God gave me difficulties
to make me strong. I asked for wisdom, and
God gave me challenges to solve.*
–Anonymous

FIREWALKING AS A TOOL FOR GROWTH

Up until 1492, most people believed that the world was flat and that if one sailed too far, he would fall off the edge. Christopher Columbus was willing to go beyond that belief, and through his direct experience, he discovered that the world is not flat. Once he returned from his voyages, that belief disappeared forever.

For most of my life, I believed that if I were to step into a glowing bed of red-hot coals measured at 1,200 degrees Fahrenheit I would burn my feet. After my first firewalk, I was never able to go back to my old belief. Because of my direct experience, that old belief was gone forever.

Beliefs are preconceived ideas through which we filter our everyday reality. In fact, we allow them to create our reality, so that what we believe about life becomes our *experience* of life. For the bio-computer we call the brain, beliefs are the software. The brain's belief system is called the Reticular Activating System (RAS). It determines how we will respond in any given situation. Our RAS is created by our religions, our teachers, our parents, and peers. Before we are five years old, it is so well formed that who we are destined to become is already determined. Anatomically, the RAS is a network of nerves radiating from the brain stem. The RAS is one of your brain's most important systems, since it determines what actually will enter your awareness. It is like the guard at the palace gates. The guard prevents trivial intrusions from disturbing the king. Likewise, the RAS, depending on how it was programmed, prevents most of the information bombarding your senses from ever making it into consciousness. Many psychologists refer to the activities of the RAS with the term *ego*. They will say something like, "You can only hear what your ego will let you hear." A limiting belief system means a limited experience of life.

Of course, beliefs and thoughts cannot be extracted from the body and examined the way bodily organs can be removed and biopsied. Yet as intangible as the mind is, it has a physical reality. The way ideas, beliefs, and decisions become tangibly manifested works like this. If you watch a scary movie, your armpits may perspire profusely—even though nothing physical is occurring. When you entertain sexual fantasies, your heart rate changes, as does your respiration, blood pressure, and body temperature. Your thoughts, your RAS, create sensation and perception.

The mind, invisible as it is, influences the brain and alters its electrochemistry. The electrochemical change is then transmitted along a series of nerves into the body, which then undergoes its own electrochemical change. Since every cell is connected to a nerve, and every nerve is connected to the brain, and the brain is influenced by the mind, it is easy to see how we create, through our beliefs and ideas, our own realities.

When you make a decision, you are programming your bio-computer, literally! Therefore, to effect meaningful change in your life, you must look at the decisions you have made. If you discover that they are limiting your experience, you must replace them with new decisions. In other words, you must reprogram how you perceive life. As Mark Twain observed, a hundred years before the mind-body connection was popularized, "Most folks are only as happy as they make up their minds to be."

OVERCOMING FEAR

In essence, this is what firewalking is all about. The fire is a metaphor for all the challenges we usually shrink from. In learning how to walk unharmed across a bed of glowing coals at a firewalk, people are really learning how to overcome fear. We learn that fear is a belief, in this case, an obstacle between where we are and where we want to go. As we step onto the coals, we pass through the membrane of fear, and in so doing, learn how to make fear our servant rather than our master.

The fire is meant to stimulate fear. And the point is not to deny the fear, but to look at it closely, to see it as something that blocks you from attaining your goal. Instead of crying about our fears and problems, blaming others, making excuses, basking in denial, or endlessly talking about them, extreme spirituality forces us to get up close with whatever is negative in our lives. That close attention enables you to gain the insight that will set you free of it.

PAY ATTENTION!

So, the first lesson in my firewalking seminar is to teach people a new way of paying attention. After all, the coals are hot, very, very hot! When striding into the coal bed, if one were to pay attention to what his head was saying about the experience, he might hear a voice shouting, "My God, your feet are being charred to stumps!" To avoid panicking at this moment, it is important to pay attention to one's feet and not one's head. What the feet say is, "Yes it is hot, but nothing is being injured. It feels much like walking barefoot on a hot street in the summer." Think about the lessons in this story:

> *A monk was being chased by a tiger. To escape, the monk lowered himself over a cliff on a long vine. Below, however, another tiger appeared. As he dangled between two deaths, several mice began chewing through the vine just above the monk's reach.*
>
> *Just then, the monk noticed a wild strawberry plant grow-ing on the side of the cliff. He plucked a strawberry and placed it in his mouth. As the vine broke, carrying the monk to his death, he gave 100 percent of his attention to the taste and texture of the berry in his mouth. By maintaining his focus on the strawberry, he avoided letting his attention wander onto the sensation of fangs and claws ripping into his body. He did indeed die; but he did not suffer.*

Life is always presenting us with tigers. Our mission is to learn how to look for the strawberries.

For example, if you are sitting in a smoke-filled restaurant, you can prevent yourself from enjoying your meal by aggravating yourself over the state of the air. The smoke is the tiger. Look for a strawberry. Perhaps there is a glorious sunset outside the window. If you focus on the sunset instead of the smoke, you can change your experience from one of suffering to one of joy. For the truth is, you are the one who creates your suffering and you are the one who creates your joy, depending on what you are doing with your consciousness.

Pay attention to what you do with your mind and you will quickly see how you create your reality—how you create your experience of life. Some teachers of consciousness believe that cultivating attentive awareness is our most important challenge. This one tool can dramatically transform a person's experience of being alive. It can make the difference between having a great life or a miserable life. Your experience of life depends on what you pay attention to. You can either enjoy a life of strawberries or feel as if you've been trapped in the tiger's den.

How often do you sit at the table watching television or reading, never really tasting the food you are eating? How frequently do you chat with your children or friends while mentally cataloging your to-do list or worrying about bills? We are all guilty of such inattentiveness. In fact, in our culture it even has a name: multitasking. But multitasking is antithetical to true awareness. Only when you are not allowing yourself to be distracted can you fully experience the richness of food in your mouth or the pleasure of others' company.

Attentive awareness is not a casual state of mind. To use it as a step toward personal power, you must pay attention to the object of your choice one hundred percent. When you do, life is transformed. When you pay attention to the smell of a flower 100 percent, you experience *becoming* the smell of the flower. When you pay attention to your dinner 100 percent, you experience *becoming* the taste of the food in your mouth. For centuries, Tantric Buddhists have applied this technique during sexual intercourse to further enhance the ecstasy of conjugation.

ATTENTIVENESS CAN MEAN LIFE OR DEATH

To help you understand the difference between paying attention 100 percent and the usual way we go through life, consider this story:

> *In an era gone by, people from all corners of the earth journeyed to see a particular wise man and ask his advice. The son of the wise man, however, was a young fellow whose mischief and disruptive ways frequently caused upsets in the community.*
>
> *Finally, out of sheer frustration at his own inability to reach the boy, the wise man sent his son to the king. The boy thus appeared before the monarch with the message that his father had sent him, hoping that the king could teach him where his father had failed.*
>
> *The king pondered for a long while, since, after all, he himself traveled often to consult with the boy's father and to seek his advice. How could he hope to teach the boy anything if the boy's own father had failed? Suddenly, the king was inspired. He looked around the huge hall and surveyed the belly dancers, the mountain of exotic food, and the assembled musicians. After a moment of thought, the king snapped his fingers, summoning two tall, muscular warriors.*
>
> *The king ordered the two warriors to stand guard on either side of the boy. He then placed a bowl of water on the youth's head. The*

bowl was filled to the brim. "Draw your swords," the sovereign com-
manded. "If this boy spills so much as one drop of water, you are to
cut off his head immediately. Don't give him time to blink an eye or
utter one word. Now take him to the circus!"

So the guards and the boy went to the circus. Jugglers and clowns
paraded among throngs of people, small children darted in all direc-
tions, merchants and food vendors hawked their wares. There were
animals roaming about, musicians, dancers, and acrobats.

Do you think the boy noticed any of it?

Of course not! All he was aware of was the bowl of water on his
head. He learned to pay attention!

How often do you pay attention like that? It is precisely this ability that can transform your life. In the story about the monk, the tigers, and the strawberry, you saw that where you focus your attention determines what you are going to experience. If you walk through a park and focus on the litter, muttering about how terrible it is to have all this garbage lying around, you won't have a very enjoyable walk. If you place your attention on the flowers, however, you may notice the litter peripheral-ly, but you have created an entirely different experience for yourself.

By the way, if you're going to pay attention to the garbage instead of the flowers, you might as well at least pick it up! A person of higher con-sciousness realizes that if you see litter and don't pick it up, it's almost the same as if you yourself put it there.

GENES DO NOT MAKE THE MAN (OR THE WOMAN)

In April of 1996, *Life* magazine profiled two conjoined twins, Abigail and Brittany. These girls are identical in their genetic makeup. Their brains are genetically the same. Because they are permanently joined, they are always in the same place, exposed to the same stimuli, at the same time. They are being educated and disciplined in the same way. You might think that, with all this, they would have identical temperaments, dispositions, and outlooks. Yet they are completely different personalities.

Because they sometimes *choose to pay attention* to different things, they are forming different memories and thus will each find different things to be important later in life. While one girl was watching television, her twin may have been gazing out the window watching a bird building a nest. Thus, the way they perceive the world around them, their experience of life, and who they become will consequently be different insofar as their intellects and personalities are concerned. So it is with us all. Our attention and how we use it is a powerful factor in determining who we become and what we are capable of doing.

So, as your first step toward personal power, begin immediately to notice where you place your attention. Consciously try to control your attentiveness. Watch your thoughts as they move through your mind as if they were quotes on a stock-market ticker tape. Pay attention to the connection between what you are thinking and how you are feeling, and where you store stress in your body.

As you cultivate this ability to pay undivided attention, you will become your own best teacher, for you'll suddenly see lessons and opportunities where you didn't even notice them before. You will be able to learn from situations you earlier had never seen. As you pay better attention, you will learn more about the people in your life and the world in which you live, in addition to learning more about yourself. Most important, by paying attention to your thoughts, you will discover how you yourself have been creating many of the problems in your life. You will discover how you yourself—not others—have created missed opportunities, and how you yourself have created separation from people who could have been of service to you. For example, a friend once locked his keys in his car. Even as he was closing the door, he later confided, a small voice was telling him that the keys were still in the ignition. Although this is a very simplistic example, it illustrates how by paying closer attention to our own thoughts, we can avoid many annoying problems that are merely a by-product of inattention.

EXPECT THE BEST

The second lesson at a firewalking seminar is learning to expect the best. When we think positive thoughts, we stimulate the production of chemicals within the brain that give us pleasurable feelings. Conversely, our negative thoughts stimulate the production of a different set of chemicals that result in discomfort. Positive thinkers are quite actually living in a different chemical environment than negative thinkers. This chemical difference alone creates a vast difference in levels of stress on the immune system. Positive thinking can be a key to vibrant health and often provides the ability to recover from injury or disease.

It is impossible to put one hundred percent of your energy into expecting the best if your head is filled with pessimistic thoughts and worry. Besides the actual thoughts themselves, another part of your energy may be spent trying to suppress those thoughts. How to get around this? We all worry. We all have negative thoughts. You don't have to eliminate them. You need to acknowledge them, address them, and even wallow in them—for a moment! Yes, before expecting the best, you must first prepare yourself for the worst. This technique is used by executives, athletes, and even astronauts in NASA's space program.

So, in any situation, ask yourself, "What is the *worst* that can possibly happen?" Go through a list of worst-case scenarios. In every one, ask yourself if you could accept it. Before I walked across a bed of glowing coals for the very first time, I considered the possibility that I might be burned. I accepted that possibility and had thought about how I would deal with it. I set the thought aside. I then proceeded to walk across the fire, expecting the best. The moment I actually stepped onto the coal bed, I was completely filling my head with positive thoughts.

Before you begin an important activity or challenge, first go through this exercise: Consider every negative scenario and emotionally prepare yourself for each and every one of those eventualities. Set each one aside after you have decided how you would deal with it. Then, when there are no longer any negative thoughts left, focus one hundred percent of your attention on a positive scenario and *expect the best!* See yourself succeeding! See yourself winning! Feel the sensations of victory before beginning the task. When you are prepared for the worst, but are expecting the best, all your bases are covered. Now you can put all your attention on the task at hand.

Sport psychologists know the importance of this strategy. In an athletic event, when a serious challenge arises, an athlete is trained never to think, "Oh, no!" That is a panic response. It prepares us for fight or flight. It is a mechanism that exists in all animals, and it is there to enable us to survive in the jungle. However, we no longer live in the jungle. Flight is not permissible on the playing field! Therefore, instead of "Oh, no!" sport psychologists encourage athletes to think, "Oh yes! Yes! This is the opportunity I have trained for! This is the challenge I have been preparing for. Yes! This is the obstacle I was meant to overcome!"

There are few rules to which there are no exceptions. Expecting the best is one. No exceptions. You always set yourself up for the best possible results when you expect the best.

Imagine, for example, you get in line to see a movie. It is a popular movie, and the line is three blocks long. When you get in line you might start thinking, "Oh gosh, I am never going to get in. I should have left earlier. It was silly of me to come on opening night. I know I won't get a seat." You continue thinking these negative thoughts, causing yourself anxiety and stress. When you finally get to the ticket booth, the person behind the glass sells you a ticket and says, "Enjoy the show." You needlessly created stress in yourself.

Doesn't it make more sense to get in line and think positive thoughts? "I know I am going to get a seat. I am looking forward to getting a big tub of buttered popcorn. I sure will enjoy telling my friends about this show tomorrow." Finally, you get to the ticket booth, and the person behind the glass says, "I'm sorry, we're sold out. There are no more seats." Are you going to say, "Damn, I just wasted a whole twenty minutes feeling good"?

Positive thinking affects your health, your relationships, and every aspect of your life. Remember, you can learn to do things with your mind that will have a significant impact on your body. The brain, the central nervous system, and the experience of being alive can all be influenced by thought. Therefore, *always* expect the best!

GO FOR IT!

To recap, the first two lessons in the firewalking seminar are to pay attention and to expect the best. The third, *Go for It!,* involves mastering the ability to attain a goal. It has four steps.

1. The first of the four steps is: know where you are. Take an honest look at yourself. Imagine you are planning to drive to a new town, one you've never been to before. You get out a map and locate the town on it. But simply knowing where that town is on the map will not help you get there, unless you also know where *you* are on the map.

2. Next, know where you want to go. Most of us don't know where we are going; we're just sure that we're not there yet. To move ahead in life purposefully and control your own reality, you must know what you want, and what experience you want to have after you have attained your goal.

3. Now, create a plan of action. Ten people can have ten different plans of action for attaining the same goal. Each can be effective. The point is to *plan.* Whether you're planning a vacation or a career change, you need plans in place before you begin. Start with your goal, where you want to be ultimately. Now work backward. For example, maybe you want to volunteer as a mentor to a child once a week for a year. But you don't even know where to begin: Who do you call? What is involved? Do I have the qualifications? Don't worry about any details yet, just start with your goal. Imagine yourself mentoring a teenager. What would be the last step you'd take before you did that? Probably you'd get some training. Where would you get the training? Probably from a social service agency. Which agency would you go to? Try calling a few local churches, or immigrant referral agencies, or the local Boys Club. In other words, start asking questions as to where you could find a mentoring program.

Soon, by working backward, you have created a plan that will get you from point A to point B. You've created a plan of action.

4. The fourth and final step to obtaining goals is simple: Follow your plan! Take the steps you devised. Revise your plans as needed, but keep your eyes on where you want to go and follow your plan.

This four-step strategy can best be summarized with three words: GO FOR IT! Here's an example. Flo moved from Ohio to California. Flo loved gardening, but was terrified of spiders. When she learned that black widow spiders live in her new state, Flo thought she would have to give up gardening.

Flo stayed indoors for several months, and then decided to tackle her fear. The first thing she did was acknowledge that she had a fear she was going to overcome. (Know where you are.) She then imagined that she would some day be able to garden again despite the black widows. Flo visualized a scene: herself among rows of corn and peas; she notices a spider and reacts calmly, as if it were a butterfly. (Know where you want to go.) Flo then devised a strategy: she bought books about spiders and a magnifying glass. She was determined to learn all she could about every spider in her area. (Create a plan of action.) Flo read about spiders and spent time watching them in their webs. (Follow your plan.) She learned that spiders bite in self-defense. They were helpful in fighting garden pests. They are beneficial! Soon, Flo *needed* spiders so that she could observe them and learn about them. She *wanted* them in her garden to help her fight insect pests.

Flo learned to go for it!

In life, as in firewalking, *Pay attention, expect the best, and go for it!* is a vehicle to success, a philosophy that holds tremendous power. It can enable you to create the reality you want. It will empower you with the body chemistry needed for success. If you internalize this simple sentence, you'll get where you want to go. It will make the difference between winning or losing. It can make the difference between sickness or recovery. With it, you begin to reprogram your attitude in a way that will empower you to attain more of your innate potential.

How else would humans have been able to run a mile in under four minutes or actually walk on the face of the moon? If you can conceive it, you can achieve it!

EXERCISE

Learning to pay attention 100 percent to your chosen object or goal is a key tool if you are to attain your full potential. As with anything, you'll need to practice in order to master the skill of attentive awareness. Try this exercise often. No one even need know that you are doing it. Sit in a chair with your eyes closed. First, pay attention to the temperature of the air on your face. Next, pay attention to the weight of the hair on your head. Then, pay attention to every subtle sound in the room around you, including sounds outside the room and sounds within your own body. As you focus your attention and awareness on the temperature, weight, or sound, be aware that you are aware. Be the watcher of your life, seeing all.

3
Skydiving
Welcoming the Tests

Thank you, Lord, for bringing me where I did not want to go.
–Nikos Kazantzakis

Extreme spirituality assumes that we do more than merely accept challenging situations. It demands that we constantly seek out challenges that will clearly reveal to us our progress on the spiritual path. It is one thing to say we have arrived at a certain place on the path; it is quite another to be able to walk our talk. Jesus said, "What does it profit a man if he has faith, but has not works? Can faith save him? Faith, if it has not works, is dead. By works a man is revealed, and not by faith alone." The "works" Jesus refers to are tests of your faith, of your willingness to take control of your path and live a life of higher consciousness.

You experience faith when watching a tightrope walker perform on a high wire. Even when the performer wiggles and sways, though you gasp, you have faith that he is not going to fall and splatter into mush and blood before your eyes. Suddenly, after the act is over, the tightrope walker comes up to you and asks you to sit on his shoulders so he can carry you along the tightrope. If you accept, much more than faith is required. At this point, faith becomes an *act of trust.*

It's these testing experiences that enable us to separate our immature ego from our more powerful conscious awareness. This is why we welcome the tests, whether the test is jumping from an airplane, walking on fire, or picking up a telephone to make an apology.

When your basic belief is that all of creation is worthy of love, you can live life in a new mode in which you seek out challenges. You trust in the perfection of all creation, with an unshakable belief that you are worthy yourself and deserve to have good experiences. Assuming that you have decided that this is the form of spirituality you want to embrace, you have already reprogrammed your bio-computer, electro-chemically, to give you what you want. This physical manifestation of your will, more than anything, takes you beyond goal setting into the realm of goal attainment.

ACKNOWLEDGING GRACE

Living in this new mode is living in a state of grace. Without this grace, it really doesn't matter what else you have. With grace, you can overcome your fears. It enables you to seek out challenges, and with your success, grace increases. When I decided to overcome my fear of heights, grace is what first enabled me to go skydiving. My sole purpose in jumping from the plane was to discover how I myself was creating my fear of heights. Even so, as I slid into the open doorway of the plane, inner voices started running through my head, "What if the parachute doesn't open? What if you get tangled in the lines? What if you don't jump out the door right? What if you don't land right?"

It suddenly became obvious to me that all these sentences began with the same two words: "What if . . ." Pay attention: perhaps this "what if" syndrome is causing many of the problems in your own life.

So right then and there, I shouted out, "Shut up!" And I jumped. In that instant, I learned not just the source of my fear of heights, but the source of all fear: in any form, fear is really linked to fear of our own mortality. I was already far enough along the spiritual path that I felt I had no real fear of dying. In fact, I had been practicing dying as often as possible. This actually had become a regular exercise for me after smashing my coconut at the temple in Sri Lanka. So what did I have to fear? Nothing! I exulted as I fell through the air. From that point on, whenever a "what if" pops up in my life, I shout, "Shut up!"

It is required that you diligently pay attention to what is going on inside your head if you are to learn how you yourself are creating your experience of life. It is especially important when you are having a negative experience.

In other words, we welcome the tests.

Remember, ego is just a filter, allowing you to experience only what ego wants you to experience. The ego, in the form of the RAS, is connected via feedback loops to every other area of the brain. So you only hear what ego lets you hear, you only see what ego lets you see, and you only think what ego will let you think. Ego is identified with the activities you do. Therefore, when you practice dying as often as possible, you come to experience that only ego dies. Only the limited you dies.

When you realize that the smashed coconut is supposed to be your head, you start imagining what the world would be like without you. Soon, you see that the world without your ego can actually be experienced without you having to die. Once the ego is set aside, the world is perceived with a clarity uncolored by ego's constantly evaluating and judging incoming data. Suddenly, there is a new perspective. There is a sense of connection to a higher power, a higher perfection, and it is reflected in everything just as it is. From this vantage point, nothing is scary or fear invoking because you perceive yourself as no longer that which can be diminished in any way.

Ego-death enables you to approach peak performance because you realize who you really are, separate from your programming. Like the dog that is aware of pain when it stubs its paw, you too are aware of pain. But unlike the dog, you are now aware that you are aware. The conscious awareness of how your ego sabotages your best intentions enables you to welcome challenges and to grow. It is this conscious awareness that ultimately provides you with freedom from fear by impartially witnessing your ego saying, "What if my parachute doesn't open?"

TESTING IS GOOD

The second time I went skydiving, a different airplane was used. The first plane had been easy to jump from: I simply had to fling my body out through an open door. The second plane was a different story: it had a wheel just beneath the door; in order to get clear of the plane, it was necessary to climb out toward the end of the wing. To do this, I had to stand on the wheel, reach up and grab the strut (the pole supporting the wing). I had to inch my way out along the strut, until I was at the edge of the wing. At that point, the jump master expected me to assume a certain posture, and then look toward him for the signal to release my hold.

Believe me, I am not James Bond. This was a tremendous challenge for me. Getting from the door of the plane to the edge of the wing involved constantly grabbing the strut, then willing myself to release it, so that I could move closer to the edge of the wing. Here I was, flapping like a piece of laundry on a clothesline, thousands of feet in the air!

The only way I was able to conquer my fear, and to let go of the strut as I inched my way along, was to repeat to myself, "Pay attention, expect the best, go for it! Pay attention, expect the best, go for it!" If that mantra could get me to the edge of that airplane's wing, I am sure it can assist you in overcoming your challenges and attaining your goals!

EXERCISE

Not all tests need to be confrontational or dramatic. Even the most mundane activities can teach us how to create our own reality.

Choose some chore or task that you dislike, such as washing your windows. As you begin, pay attention to what you tell yourself. Observe the effect that your thoughts have on the way you feel, the amount of energy you have, and the level of joy or disgust you're experiencing. Pay attention to the water, to the smooth motion of your hand across the glass, to the reflection of the blue sky and clouds behind you. Look for the pleasure in the moment.

As you pay attention, you will discover how you yourself create your experience with the very thoughts you allow or disallow. When you notice disempowering and negative thoughts inside your head, learn to shout in your head two very powerful words: "Shut up!"

4

Allowing an Object to Pass through Your Body
Redefining What's Possible

*We haven't begun to understand the power that God has
created within the human being and within life.*
–Reverend Robert Schuller

As intense as skydiving was, a greater test for me involved piercing my
own body with a five-inch needle. When Geraldo Rivera called me to do
a show on firewalking, I invited several other people onto the show to
help round out the presentation on using challenges to facilitate growth.
Sitting next to me onstage was a fellow who demonstrated pushing a five-
inch quilting needle through his hand without pain or bleeding. Since I
had an aversion to needles, I wasn't too happy being seated right next to
this guy. However, television cameras were broadcasting the show
nationwide, so I feigned interest in watching a needle penetrate a human
hand and emerge on the other side.

Despite my disgust, what struck me was that the man's face was literally shining. Not only wasn't he grimacing, he was in bliss. I felt instantly
compelled to experience the mystery that created this bliss. I recognized
that my aversion to putting a needle through my hand was a needed lesson

for personal growth. Like many of the exercises in my seminars, the needle was very dramatic. I like this kind of drama, as it makes certain lessons more memorable, more indelible. Being able to remember a lesson is oftentimes all that is needed to be rescued from a painful moment.

So I eventually introduced pushing a needle through the hand as a dramatic exercise in my seminars to help participants redefine what they thought was possible. Like firewalking, the needle became a metaphor to help people look at all kinds of limiting issues.

Some people passed out cold just *watching* the process. Others threw up. Interestingly, the fainters and vomiters never even got close to the needle. Obviously, what caused their distress was not physical pain, but emotional.

These kinds of tests empower us. We discover how our minds work and can use these new and empowering states of awareness to transform the way we interact with life. We see that pain, just like a bed of coals, represents a limiting situation, and we are given the opportunity to learn how we create the results we don't want so that we can effectively make the internal changes that will enable us to create the results we do want.

The truly remarkable aspect of this process goes beyond the fact that it can be done without pain and without bleeding; it is in the bliss it generates in the participants. Bliss is a state of consciousness that is literally beyond words. Simply put, it is egolessness. At one seminar, every single participant put the needle through his/her hand, and the bliss became so intense that people leapt to their feet and spontaneously began to dance. Fortunately, it's documented on videotape, and it's quite amazing to witness people's minds actually getting blown away just from watching the video! This is why you too can have a transformational experience from simply reading this book. There are times when we ourselves don't necessarily have to participate in something extreme but can be profoundly affected just by witnessing it or listening to someone else relate the experience. Haven't you ever been inspired by someone else's courage? Watching another person overcome a formidable obstacle or challenge can give the watcher a vicarious experience that results in a permanent change in the witness, though he or she goes through the entire process in the comfort of an armchair.

LET IT BE EASY

Do you limit yourself by saying, in any given situation, "This will be hard" or "This will be difficult"? That was the problem I needed to overcome. The needle, I knew, could help me.

At first, I would sit with the needle pressed against my skin, but every time I went to push, something paralyzed me and I became a frozen stone. Sweat broke out on my forehead, and try as I would, I could not will my hand to push with the thrust necessary to put the needle through one side of my hand and out the other.

I prayed for strength. Deep within me, I heard, "Let it be easy."

Easy!? How could this ever be easy?

Again came the quiet counsel from within, "Let it be easy."

Actually, it had never even occurred to me that this could be easy.

"Let it be easy." "Let it be easy."

As perspiration dripped from my brow I pushed! To my amazement, the needle slid through my hand like a warm knife through butter. No pain whatsoever. There was no blood. None!

The skin all over my body began to tingle, and the hair on the back of my neck stood up. I could barely catch my breath. The experience was not unlike an orgasm. I was in bliss! If I had not experienced this myself it would have been impossible for me to believe. More than any other challenge described in this book, pushing a needle through my hand has to stand out as the most difficult victory I've achieved. As a result, the lessons gleaned from this are more vital and valuable for me personally than any of the insights I've received from other exercises. I saw so clearly how I needed to stop telling myself in advance that certain activities were going to be difficult.

FREEDOM FROM THE KNOWN

Whether you push a needle through your hand or not, if you are willing to break free from your own limiting ego states (like, "This is too hard for me," or "I can't," or "He can, but not me"), you will begin to see what is really going on with yourself; not just what your ego wants you to see. You'll begin to experience reality—not the reality filtered through your limiting RAS but the reality that is open to all possibilities.

Here's an example of how the RAS can limit your opportunities:

> A priest was trapped in a flood. When the water begins to cover the roof of his house, he climbed up onto the chimney. A man in a passing rowboat shouted, "Come aboard!"
>
> "Save someone of lesser faith," the priest replied, "God will save me." Another rowboat approached. Another opportunity to get down off the chimney was rejected. Finally a helicopter came and dropped a rope to the

clinging priest. But he again refused and ultimately drowned.

In heaven, the priest asked, "God, why didn't you save me?" God replied, "You dummy! I sent you two rowboats and a helicopter!"

After you get free from the false perceptions of your ego, you will no longer see *rowboats* and *helicopters,* rather you will see opportunities to grow and discover that God and the potential for bliss can be everywhere. Certainly Jesus wasn't crying about the pain those nails were creating in his hands and feet. On the cross, Jesus was able to say: *Forgive them.*

Pay attention! Life is a mirror that will constantly reflect back to you where you are in your spiritual development and give you opportunities to move forward. If you want to know what your beliefs are that create your life, pay attention to what is inside your head! To a large extent, you create your experiences. If you aren't happy, you may not be able to change the situation, but you possess a power that no one else has: the power to change how you choose to react.

Learn to say to your inner, limiting voices, "Shut up!" And then to say, "Let it be easy."

There is no practical advantage to putting a needle through your hand. It's not a skill you'll need too often in life. But these kinds of tests can empower you. We discover how our minds work and can use these new and empowering states of awareness to transform the way we interact with the people and events in our lives. We see that our suffering, just like a bed of coals or a five-inch needle, represents a limiting situation. Just as when we're given a chance to triumph over the needle, each day we are given the opportunities to see how we limit ourselves. Once we see, we can make the internal changes that will enable us to create the results we want in life.

Perhaps you volunteer for a project at your child's school. Once all the ramifications of the work become obvious to you, you might feel overwhelmed by the vastness of the tasks involved. If you catch yourself saying things like, "This is more than I bargained for," or "I'll never be able to complete this on time," substitute the phrase "This can be easy." Notice how doubt depletes your energy, but the willingness to let something be easy actually gives you the needed energy to complete the chore.

EXERCISE

Write the words *Let it be easy!* on several three-by-five-inch index cards. Tape one on your bathroom mirror. Put another card on your refrigerator. Stick one on the dashboard of your car. Slip another card into your wallet.

Over the span of the next few days, notice how you make things difficult by telling yourself certain activities are hard. Then think about how you can change that perception. Tell yourself that compared to childbirth, this is a piece of cake.

Consciously look at the cards each day. Let them remind you that you have the ability to experience things in a different mode than you have in the past. You will see how resisting certain actions actually creates more stress than learning ways to harmonize. You begin learning life's lessons from your own insights. In other words, you become your own teacher. No one will be able to accuse you of missing the rowboat.

5

Using Slot Machines as Biofeedback Devices
Awakening through the Unconventional

*We don't need to fully comprehend the concept of
consciousness to appreciate its value. Just our willingness
to consider the vastness of ourselves, our unlimitedness, our
infinite potential, is sufficient to infuse us with a
sense of our magnificence.*
–Arnold Patent

My brand of extreme spirituality has led to some unusual exercises in my self-empowerment seminars. Firewalking, skydiving, and five-inch needles may seem extreme, but as you can now see, only when taken out of context. Likewise, the fact that I use casinos as a venue for many of my spiritual seminars might also seem preposterous. However, I seek the unconventional because my purpose is always to quicken people's awakening.

Believe it or not, a casino provides the perfect setting to experience a state of grace. As a venue for spiritual growth, it is as radical and extreme as a needle or coal bed. A slot machine can actually be used as a biofeedback device to help you gain a more intimate connection with love and with God. After all, slot machines are run by the same divine energy that runs everything else in the universe!

Slot machines, as outrageous as it might seem, are a powerful vehicle to help you learn how to keep your heart open. Remember how our attitudes affect our body chemistry? Since the brain and, in fact, the entire body, is a package of electrochemical impulses, it shouldn't seem so far-fetched that we can influence electronic devices.

However, casinos and slot machines are not the right venue for your spiritual growth if you have a history or tendency toward addiction of any kind. Here we use slot machines as a tool toward personal growth, toward a more spiritual reality. Others use them to avoid reality of any kind, and instead of a tool, they can become a destructive force.

GRACE

Grace is, among its other definitions, "a sense of fitness or propriety," and "divine love and protection freely bestowed on humanity." To me, grace is a tangible manifestation of God's love for me. For most of us, grace appears uninvited and unacknowledged. But you can greatly amplify the presence of grace in your life if you see yourself as deserving of it; you invite it in, you acknowledge it, and give thanks for it.

To demonstrate how to increase grace in your life, I frequently bring groups to Nevada casinos. There I tell them a true story about my friend Roger, a medical doctor working in a hospital emergency room. One day an ambulance delivered a man who had just suffered a bizarre string of accidents.

The man was in his mid-fifties and had been driving his large RV into a remote and very steep canyon. It was a dry September day in the Sierra foothills. Without warning, the RV's brakes failed. In an effort to stop the big rig, the man turned his wheels toward the canyon wall. However, instead of stopping him, the impact caused the RV to bounce off the canyon wall and roll over into the canyon. It rolled over and over as it careened into the steep gorge. As it rolled, large sections of the vehicle's body were shorn from the chassis, and by the time it landed on the floor of the canyon, nothing remained but the man himself, belted to the seat that remained attached to the metal chassis. The RV landed upright and the man, though seriously shaken, was not badly hurt. He released his safety belt and began to run from the scene when, suddenly, the gas tank exploded. The explosion instantly ignited the tinder-dry canyon, and a wildfire was soon raging in the forest. The man scrambled up the stony cliff, barefoot and without a shirt.

He had just stopped on a sheer rock outcropping to catch his breath when the pine tree above him burst into flames and began raining flaming branches down upon him. He narrowly escaped being burned and climbed again upwards toward the top. By now, the California Department of Forestry had deployed an air tanker, and just as the man reached the road, he was bombed with fire-retarding borate.

Gasping, he made his way along the road and soon encountered a fire crew, who called the ambulance. Roger examined him in the emergency room and found the man to be basically unharmed. He suffered a fractured rib and a multitude of superficial lacerations and bruises.

There were clearly at least half a dozen times this man could have been killed or severely injured. As he escaped each of these moments, grace was bestowed on him. Whether or not this man ever acknowledges it, it remains what it is. Some may want to dismiss grace when it appears in their lives or try to explain it away by labeling it a mere coincidence. Extreme spirituality calls us to acknowledge the grace in our lives and continually offer gratitude for it.

The more you acknowledge grace, and say "thank you" for moments of grace, the more it will appear in your life, as if attracted by a magnet. A good way to begin this process is by saying to yourself: *God loves me. I deserve God's love.* In that moment, all unworthiness, guilt, and embarrassment dissolve instantly. It is similar to the way walking on fire removes a lifetime of programming.

MONEY AS A METAPHOR

Back to the casino. Since slot machines are meant to pay jackpots (no one would come if they never paid out), acknowledging the grace in your life means that you no longer proceed from the premise that someone else will win rather than you, or that someone else is more deserving. You begin living with the awareness that you deserve to be a winner. For the sake of this casino exercise, you have to allow yourself to receive God's love (grace) in the form of money.

The money becomes a metaphor for love. The entire process of using the slot machine as a biofeedback device is constructed so you can examine your issues about guilt and unworthiness, and learn how the ego creates your reality. When you learn to ask for and to accept grace, the money (or love) comes.

As with firewalking, the lessons learned in a casino seminar become tools by which to live. People learn to say thank you for everything in their lives, because within every experience, especially negative ones, lies an opportunity for grace and for growth.

Living daily with an awareness of grace and with an attitude of gratitude doesn't happen to you overnight. It's a matter of learning how to use a spiritual muscle. New attitudes, like untrained muscles, take time to develop. You don't leave the gym with bulging muscles after one visit. But if you go regularly, in time you see a change. It is the same with grace. If you want it in your life, make the decision to exercise your grace awareness. In time, the grace in your life will be as obvious to you as the bulging muscles on a regular gym rat.

EXPERIENCING ABUNDANCE BY OPENING YOUR HEART

The state of the universe is one of *abundance*. We don't have to do anything to create this abundance; we simply need to be aware of it. If there is *something* we need to *do,* it is to recognize *how we are cutting ourselves off from this abundance that exists everywhere in the universe.* Ramana Maharshi said, "Of what use is it to complain of the stinginess of the ocean if you approach holding only a thimble?"

I have learned that when I am closing my heart, I am cutting myself off not only from the *abundance* of the universe but from the potential *love* that exists everywhere as well. And slot machines can be used as biofeedback devices to help us gain a more intimate connection with love and with God.

As outrageous as this might seem, I've found this tool to be the most powerful vehicle I've known in learning how to keep my heart open. Earlier, I spoke about the difference in body chemistry when we are thinking negative thoughts versus when we are thinking positive thoughts. The electrochemical state we are generating with our thoughts not only affects our own bodies, but what occurs around us.

Today, slot machines are controlled by a computer chip known as a Random Event Generator (REG). A Texas physicist, Helmut Schmidt, has conducted experiments to see whether or not we could influence the REG with our minds. His research at the University of Texas over the past twenty years has yielded conclusive results that we can impact the computer chip using nothing more than thought.

So, if a person believes someone else will surely win the jackpot, rather than him/herself, the machine will respond to that. The same thought patterns that tell us we are worthy of tremendous wealth, or *not*, are the same thought patterns that determine whether we experience love and an open heart, or the opposite. If we do not feel worthy of wealth, we do not feel worthy of any other good thing as well.

By paying attention to our thoughts while sitting in front of a slot machine, we can find out what it is we do with our minds that keeps us cut off from receiving grace and love.

Despite years of spiritual exploration, it was the slot machine, used as a biofeedback device, that finally helped me discover what it was I was doing with my thoughts that determined whether my heart was open or closed. I sat in front of the slot machine and closed my eyes. I paid attention to my mind, my body, and the sensations in my chest around my heart. With my eyes closed, I would do mental exercises in an effort to open my heart.

I experimented, visualizing angels, calling upon Jesus, even imagining that I was Jesus. I practiced forgiveness, offered gratitude for grace, sang silent hymns, laughed, and cried. At the moment when I thought my heart was open, I would put a coin in the slot machine and pull the handle. If money came out, that indicated my heart was indeed open and a cause for celebration and joy. If nothing came out, that was a signal to work a little more. No way to lose!

I discovered how easy it is to fool oneself into thinking that the heart is open when it really isn't. Or perhaps the heart is open, but merely a crack, with reservations, and we delude ourselves into thinking it is wide open.

I started experimenting with other thoughts and techniques to see which were the most effective at helping me maintain an open heart. When I was experiencing appreciation, the machine yielded money. When I was experiencing gratitude, again the machine confirmed that this was a doorway to the open heart. I was quite moved emotionally. At one point I began weeping. I am sure everyone who passed me assumed I had lost all my money in the slot machine!

Enough experimentation, I decided. Time to put my theory to the test with an ongoing struggle I was having. I decided to process my relationship with my former wife using a slot machine. I began forgiving her for all the incidents that I had been holding onto for so long. I released all pettiness. I began to appreciate those qualities in her that are extraordinary.

After working for about fifteen minutes, I felt that I had opened my heart completely, and I put a coin in the slot machine. I pulled the handle. Nothing happened!

Perhaps I was fooling myself. I began to look deeper. Sure enough, there were still petty incidents I was holding onto. I worked for another ten minutes. When I was certain that I had completely opened my heart and come into a place of unconditional love, I again put in a quarter and pulled the handle. Nothing happened.

"Hmm, what's going on here?"

Then inspiration struck: I would give 10 percent of any jackpot to my former wife. Now certainly that was a demonstration that my heart was open. Again I put in the coin and pulled the handle. Again, nothing. This caused me to go deeper and deeper. Where was I holding onto resentment? Where was I not in 100 percent alignment with love?

LOVE IS AN ACTION VERB

Then I realized that what I called love was too passive. Love is an activity; it requires action.

I also realized that I was still subtly holding onto some anger. I could *say* I loved my former wife, but did I *really* want her to win in life? Did I want her to be inundated with abundance? Did I want her to have fulfillment, prosperity, and success? I realized that I was hiding the answer from myself, because there, concealed within a dark corner of my mind, the answer was no. I didn't really want her to win; not as much as I wanted myself to win.

A part of me was still competing with her. A part of me was trapped in jealousy, and so of course the machine paid nothing. If I gave 10 percent of nothing to my ex-wife, she would wind up with nothing. In a subtle way, I discovered that I really didn't want her to get the money I had promised to give her from the jackpot.

I could fool myself, but I couldn't fool the slot machine. It, like everything else in the universe, was an expression of God. When I sat in front of the slot machine, I was in an egoless relationship with the divine. The machine had no judgments, no programming, no ego of its own. It was an empty mirror reflecting everything within myself.

The machine never hurried me. I was allowed to take as much time as I needed. I closed my eyes and suddenly was alone with God. There was no longer a casino around me. I no longer heard the clanging of slot machine bells or smelled the pungent odor of cigarette smoke in the air. I was removed to a tranquil place.

Within that stillness, I finally was able to ferret out every obstacle keeping me from opening my heart completely to my ex-wife. I opened my eyes and realized that I actually did want her to win in life. If she wasn't winning, then our daughter, Amber, would never win. And if Amber didn't win, I couldn't win.

I decided it did not matter what happened with the slot machine; I was going to help my daughter's mother win in life. I would commit myself to being a support for her. I took out my checkbook and wrote her a large check. Regardless of what happened with the slot machine, I would give it to her. In went a coin, down went the handle, and of course, out came a jackpot!

Writing the check—an act of love—was the action I needed to take to truly open my heart.

Here's where paying attention is so crucial. At that moment, I paid attention, very, very close attention, to what I had been doing that opened my heart so wide. I never wanted to forget what it was that I was aiming for in life and I wanted a frame of reference that would make it easier for me to open my heart in the future.

The slot machine became an exercise in experiencing love, and also an exercise in experiencing grace. I've used it to work on guilt I carried through adulthood, guilt over things I had done while still in childhood.

One of the first things we have to do when using the slot machine as a biofeedback device is practice forgiveness. Not just forgiveness toward others, but also forgiveness for ourselves.

Isn't it time you gave up all your self-judgments so that you can feel worthy of receiving love, prosperity, grace, and joy? If not now, when?

YOU DESERVE TO BE A WINNER

I once began a casino seminar by announcing that the entire group would be going skydiving together. We were not, in fact, going skydiving. I simply said that to get a reaction. Half of the group was excited by the idea, assuming that they were going to be safe. There was no fear in them. It never occurred to them that they wouldn't have a wonderful experience. However, the other half of the group was petrified because they doubted whether they would be safe. A part of them thought perhaps their parachute wouldn't open.

As we explored both lines of thinking, it quickly became apparent that the people in the first group felt they deserved joy, success, and love. As a result, they were open to whatever the universe presented. Those in the second group felt they weren't worthy of God's love. They also felt, it turned out, that they didn't feel they deserved wealth either. How about you? Which group are you in?

When people don't feel they deserve abundance, they live in some degree of fear. It is important we follow the thoughts that create our experience of fear. That's how to discover why we feel inadequate, why we push away the abundance that is always around us.

True wealth is not money. It is comfort, safety, peace, freedom, and ease. These feelings are a natural by-product of an open heart. They are a gift of grace.

Once the heart is open wide, true wealth follows. I learned my own pettiness usually prevented me from keeping my heart open at all times. To be free of pettiness, to live in a state of grace and constant love, is in fact the wealth that I had always wanted.

There, in Las Vegas, I began forming a new paradigm about wealth. For many years I believed that if I worked hard, and if I saved conscientiously, eventually I would have wealth. I was a true product of a capitalistic system. A better paradigm is that we are always being taken care of. We still have to work and be productive, but with a sense of abundance, not of scarcity. Within this new paradigm, you can indeed relax and feel comfort, safety, peace, freedom, and ease—true wealth.

Once you firmly root yourself in this new paradigm, you don't need a slot machine to reveal how you are keeping your heart closed. You live from your heart rather than your head, and know what the difference feels like. You'll find that your body itself is a good signal to point out whether or not your heart is open. When your body is tense, you're in your head. When you're in your heart, your body is relaxed. So use your body for feedback to help you keep your heart wide open. Just being aware of the times when you're not in your heart is the beginning of the process for getting back into it.

Slot machines are merely one window of opportunity to experience grace. You will discover that windows of opportunity are open everywhere once you begin looking for them.

RESPONDING WITH LOVE

I have been working on keeping my heart open for many years now, and I'd like to share a simple scenario, one you've probably experienced, that shows how it works. One day I was out driving, feeling particularly joyful and exalted. My heart was open, and the world seemed magnificent.

I stopped at a gas station. I went inside before pumping the gas, because there was a sign saying you needed to leave your card with the attendant. I gave her my Visa card and went outside to fill my tank. When I came back in, the clerk told me that they did not take Visa, only ATM cards.

Immediately, I felt myself flip into an adversarial position. I was about to snap at the clerk, "What if I hadn't had an ATM card? Why didn't you tell me before I pumped the gas that you wanted an ATM card?" Instead, luckily, I heard the voice of grace: "Is this worth closing your heart for?" The answer was sudden and clear: of course not! I said nothing, reached into my pocket, took out some cash, and paid for the gas.

And that is the question to ask yourself: *Is this worth closing my heart for?* Try it the next time you get angry. *Is this worth closing my heart for?*

The more you live in a state of love, grace, and an open heart, the more unacceptable you'll find it when your heart is closed. As soon as you begin realizing there is nothing worth closing your heart for, that's how soon your life can be transformed by love. It is simply a matter of taking responsibility for keeping your heart open.

There are always going to be negative life situations. Some are trivial, like a surly clerk. Others, such as the death of a loved one, illness, or injustice, can bring a sadness that seems insurmountable. You have no control over many of these situations, but you do have control over how you'll respond to them. If you decide to respond with an open heart, you can experience heaven right here on earth, even with all its seeming imperfections.

For many years, I was angry and resentful about a car accident that physically changed my life forever. Now I realize I was given a difficult experience so I could become who it is I am becoming. I am grateful for that accident. It motivated me to become a more spiritual person. And indirectly, it was responsible for me discovering life's most profound teachings.

How do you come to this place of gratitude and acceptance? Sometimes it's not so difficult. Other situations, such as the death of a child, are so difficult it can take years to reach this place. Following are some strategies to help keep your heart open.

Consciously send blessings to people. Sit quietly, close your eyes, visualize the person's face who has hurt you, and consciously beam them love and blessings.

Or close your eyes and visualize your heart. Visualize it growing larger and larger. Visualize that it is so large that it actually encompasses the room you are in. Enlarge it still further, to encompass the entire neighborhood. And finally, let your heart become so large that it encompasses the entire planet. By doing this you will find that every situation can be encompassed in love. Visualization is a powerful technique; it allows you to bring about those chemical changes in the brain that can give you a better physical experience here on Earth.

WALK YOUR TALK

Put your decision to change your life into action. Make a list of everything you're grateful for. Write a forgiveness list. Forgive yourself. Pick litter off the streets. (I guarantee you will feel better about yourself after having done that.) The more you put your philosophy into action, the more you will start sensing that you are a loved, cared for, and responsible member of creation.

Rational understanding is not enough. Like learning how to drive with a clutch, no matter how many books you read about it, it's not until you actually sit behind the wheel that you grasp the process. When you change your theoretical understanding into physical action, that's when understanding becomes realization.

Athletes say, "Fake it till you make it." Use the same strategy on your spiritual path. Tell yourself you are not going to fret about money for a while; you're going to trust that your life is and will continue to be filled with abundance. You'll notice a peace and ease that comes along with this kind of thinking.

As you recognize the grace flowing into your life, remember to say thank you. Cultivate a perpetual state of gratitude.

There are always going to be tests of your decision to see life as filled with abundance, grace, and love. Those are your challenges. Life should not always be easy. It's the challenges that motivate us to grow. If you are not willing to be pushed, you will never find out how far you can go . . . how far you can grow.

Paraphrasing what Jesus said, it is easy to love people when they are being nice to you. The challenge, of course, is to be loving when people are not so nice to you.

It is easy to have faith when there's money in the bank. The challenge is to feel that same degree of safety and abundance when the account hovers around zero . . . knowing that everything moves in cycles. The pendulum can only go so far in one direction before it has to swing back in the other direction again.

Constantly choose the experience you want in any given situation. For example, it takes two people to argue. If one person makes a conscious decision not to participate, there can be no argument.

PAY ATTENTION! PAY ATTENTION! PAY ATTENTION!

The ability to make conscious decisions to choose your own experience comes from paying attention. Of course, there will be times when you're going to blow it. You think you're paying attention, but suddenly you step in dog shit. Instead of beating yourself up, just say, "Oh, there is a reminder. I need to pay attention a little bit more when I'm walking down the street." It is an opportunity to say, "Thank you for reminding me to pay attention."

Once you make this paradigm shift, everything becomes an opportunity for growth. Even dog shit.

IT'S NEVER TOO LATE TO LIVE A LIFE OF LOVE

A stone may have been lying at the bottom of a riverbed for ten million years, but if you pluck it out and set it in the sun, in five minutes it is dry. If you take a dry stone from the bank and swish it in the water for just two seconds, put it down to dry again, then a moment after, you will not be able to tell the difference between the two stones. The one that was wet for millions of years is just as dry now as the stone that was only wet for a few seconds.

Your future doesn't reflect your past. No matter how long you have been living a loveless life, once you set an intention to make this shift into a new paradigm, once you attain this new way of being, the quality of your life can change forever. Love newly found is exactly the same as love in someone who has been living with love for decades.

The more love you give, the more you have. You can never exhaust the amount of love you have. If you are holding a lit candle, one hundred people can come to you with unlit candles, place theirs in your flame, and walk away with a flame of their own. Even after giving one hundred people some of your flame, yours is not diminished.

THE PROCESSIONAL EFFECT

Buckminster Fuller first described what he called the processional effect, or starting out on what seems to be one journey but winding up on another journey completely.

Imagine you get up in the morning to make coffee and find there is no cream. So you get into your car, figuring you'll run to the 7-11 to get some. On the way, you look up and notice a magnificent rainbow stretching from horizon to horizon. You're so moved by its beauty that you pull the car over so you can better appreciate the rainbow.

Just then, you notice, next to the road, a meadow of wildflowers. You're so smitten by the moment that a poem pops into your mind. You pick up a pencil and paper, walk out into the meadow, sit down, and begin composing poetry. Hours pass and you are suddenly aware that you forgot to get the cream for your coffee.

When you got in your car, you thought you were going to buy cream for your coffee. In fact, you were going to drive yourself to a meadow of wildflowers so you could compose poetry.

The processional effect reminds us that we never truly know where we are going. That's why it is important to *pay attention* along the way, because you can receive gifts from the universe at the most unlikely and unexpected moments.

PAIN CAN CARRY GRACE

Let go of any idea of what form grace must take. Sometimes it may look like suffering. Much of my emotional pain was actually good pain. It was emotional garbage that I had been stashing deep down inside myself for a long, long time. As I was willing to grow, this pain came up, and it was necessary to experience it as it was being released.

If you experience something similar, don't push that pain back down when it arises, because then you'll be holding onto it. It is a little bit like a barrel of old crankcase oil. Imagine pouring clear water into the barrel. Suddenly, all of the yucky oil comes up to the surface. When it comes up, it is on its way out. As long as you keep pouring water into the barrel, eventually that oil will spill out and be gone. However, if you push the oil back down, because you don't want to see it, then it's going to remain in the barrel. You have to be willing to let it surface so that it can be released.

Letting pain surface is hard. You start working on yourself, start focusing on love and light, and suddenly you are in so much pain it is almost unbearable. You are looking for joy and healing, and when the pain comes up, you can get confused. Just remember that pain can be a part of the process. Allow it to come up, experience it fully, and release it.

THE POWER IN MAKING A DECISION

So I hope you'll decide to live with your heart open. Recognize that there is tremendous power just in making that decision. It doesn't matter what the decision is about, relationships or money or career, once you make a decision, you have actually used your mind to reprogram your bio-computer.

Making a decision is like drawing a line in the sand; you're either on this side or you're on that side. Spiritual growth starts with making a decision.

The prospect of shifting into a new paradigm can be scary. When my daughter, Amber, was five years old, we were rappelling down a 200-foot cliff. As we were getting started, she said, "Daddy, I'm really scared," and she started to cry.

I said, "Sweetie, it's OK, you don't have to do this."

She retorted, with dignity, "Daddy, I said I was scared. I didn't say I didn't want to do it."

Amber stopped crying and descended the cliff. Later, she told me that the rappel was one of the most exhilarating things she had ever done. At a very early age, Amber made a decision to develop her full potential. She takes risks and she accepts challenges. She often goes way beyond her comfort zone, even when it is scary. I am frequently empowered simply by witnessing the courage and wisdom in my daughter.

May you also be empowered by what Amber taught me: "Just because I'm scared doesn't mean I'm not going to do it."

EXERCISE

Close your eyes. Visualize yourself paying your bills at your desk or table. Still with eyes closed, imagine turning around and discovering a magical staircase that leads down to a closed door. Pretend you are descending the stairs. Open the door and step through it. You are now standing in a holy place. Feel the temperature of the air in this sanctuary. Listen to the stillness. Notice the aura of sanctity everywhere you look.

Now open your eyes and remember the feelings created in the sanctuary. Notice how different it felt to be in a holy place than when you were paying the bills.

Pay attention to the fact that there is a different physical sensation when you are in your head versus being in your heart. Notice the difference so you can monitor yourself as you go through the coming days and honestly observe how much time you spend in your head and how much time you spend in your heart.

6
Breaking Boards and Bricks with Your Bare Hand
Bursting the Limits of Your Ego

Our self-perception determines our behavior. If we think we're small . . . we tend to behave that way. If we think we're magnificent . . . we tend to behave that way.
—Marianne Williamson

Virginia attended one of my seminars on peak performance. She was seventy years old, frail, and had a slight tremor. Using some of the techniques in this book, she was able to break a brick with her bare hand after about ten minutes of instruction.

I teach people to break boards and bricks with their bare hands to demonstrate how the ego continually limits us. The ego would have us think that only someone extensively trained in martial arts can break boards and bricks. Before breaking the brick, Virginia had already broken a board, which was, of course, a bit easier. As she approached the brick, she hesitated. "I don't know if I can do this," she began, "but I'll try."

In that moment, the ego revealed how it interferes with peak performance and ultimate success. As a result of the way Virginia's brain had been programmed, her RAS, her ego, was about to determine how she would perceive and respond to this situation. This ego response would then determine how much energy she would have.

Ego controls energy. For example, a man comes home from work absolutely exhausted. He has no energy. A friend phones requesting help moving some furniture and the man responds, "Not tonight, I have no energy." Moments later, his girlfriend phones to tell him she's throwing a spontaneous party and wants him to spend the night with her afterward. "I'll be right over," he replies instantly.

If we label a task as disagreeable, ego limits our energy. Conversely, when something agreeable comes into our lives, suddenly ego is able to liberate huge amounts of energy. The man's first response was 100 percent true. He wasn't lying. He simply had no energy.

The RAS is akin to a computer's software. Like the old programmer's axiom of GIGO (garbage in, garbage out), changes made to your RAS, to your perceptions, manifest themselves in the quality of your life—good or bad. Virginia had to see that the word "try" implies room for failure. Try aims for an attempt, rather than a result. Her thoughts were imbued with doubt. Had she struck the brick in that state, she would certainly have hurt her hand.

By being willing to pay attention and see her reactions impartially as a viewer of her ego, Virginia saw how her ego influenced how she approached the brick. Like the other examples of obstacles—needles, coal beds—the brick is a metaphor. It represents every situation in your life where you give less than 100 percent or shrink back because you feel intimidated. With awareness, the brick can become merely an obstacle between you and your goal. It is not a negative situation. It is a challenge.

EXAMINE YOUR PROGRAMMING

When approaching a challenge, step one is to pay attention to the programming your RAS is running. If it is fear, welcome the opportunity to see how your fear is constructed so you can reshape it into something more effective. If you deny the existence of your fears and anxieties, you'll miss the first step toward eliminating them. How can you make something go away if you aren't willing to admit it is there in the first place?

Then, once you acknowledge your fear, shut down the limiting program. Do this by simply shouting at it, "Shut up!" You can shout internally or externally. (This is voice-recognition software . . . no keyboards are required!)

Lastly, create some new programming with which you want the ego to operate: I can do this! I will do this! I must do this! Virginia began visualizing her fist eight inches below the brick. Herein lies the secret. By aiming well below the brick, i.e., *past* the challenge, and affirming that 100 percent of your strength will be used for power, you approach the challenge with absolute confidence. This enables you to use all your strength to bring your fist into the intended position, which is on the other side of the brick.

If you approach the brick with any doubt, you will, of course, slow down as you see your hand approaching it. After all, you don't want to hurt your hand (ego speaking). Yet, if you slow down or pull back in any way, you will hurt your hand and the brick won't break. Though this particular test may seem inordinately intense, it is really not. When striking the brick at its exact center, it doesn't take as much physical strength as you might imagine. When struck with a powerful blow at dead center, the brick seems to literally separate and the sensation is more like feeling your hand pass through something instead of into something.

With absolute focus and determination, Virginia finally split her brick in two using one quick blow from the palm of her hand.

YOUNG CHILDREN BREAKING BOARDS

I demonstrate the power of reprogramming ego in schools, using boards. There is minimal risk, perhaps a scrape or a small bruise if a child doesn't use enough force and the board just won't break. In schools, I also employ a face-saving ritual that includes using a tool for a power assist. (The board always yields to a smash from a giant hammer!)

In one fifth-grade class, each of the twenty-four children had successfully broken a board using just their bare fists, with the exception of Jenny, a shy and withdrawn girl who was quite thin, with forward-sloping, rounded shoulders. When I passed out the boards, Jenny refused to even take one.

Through gentle coaxing, Jenny finally accepted a board after everyone else had broken theirs. Her classmates were exuberant over their successes and flooded Jenny with positivity. "We are with you, Jen," a boy said. "At least try," another classmate urged. I immediately interrupted and shared Virginia's story and the moral of Virginia's story: *Don't try, just do it.*

"I know I can't do it," Jennifer insisted. So I explained more about the RAS and programming. If you say "I can't," then you are programmed so that you will never consider succeeding in a certain arena and therefore won't even enter the arena. So, of course, you can't do whatever it is you decided not to do.

I told Jenny that I would never have suggested to her that she accept this challenge if I myself had any doubt she could succeed. I gave her a chance to bow out gracefully by saying, "I know you can do this, Jenny. And as soon as you know it too, you will do it. Perhaps today isn't the appropriate day for whatever reason."

With that, Jenny got out of her seat, went to the center of the room where two cinder blocks stood, placed her board between them, and smashed the board to pieces with her bare hand. Her classmates went nuts with hoots and cheers. Jenny's posture instantly changed. Instead of being round-shouldered, her rib cage swelled, her chin lifted, and her shoulders relaxed into an upright, open position. She was grinning so hard her face looked transfigured.

In that moment, a brief but direct experience wiped out a lifetime of programming for young Jenny.

As the story of the tightrope walkers reminds us, we first move into faith, then into trust, then into action. Most of the people with whom I work are already into faith. Jenny, however, demonstrated exceptional progress, as she wasn't even into faith when I met her.

LOOKOUT FOR DOUBT

Before I made these kinds of changes in my life, I always approached formidable challenges with doubt. My usual mode was: I can't do this . . . I can't do that . . .

After learning to recognize how my ego was limiting me, I adopted the affirmation, I can do anything! In this way, my RAS became reprogrammed. And yet, I do not choose to walk on every fire, and I sometimes elect not to undertake certain challenges. For a part of the process is to know that every time there is a challenge, you are a new person. Since change is our nature, it isn't always appropriate for me to do something today that I might have done only three days before.

As you approach each challenge in life, run different scenarios through your mind. See yourself accepting the challenge and also see yourself declining the challenge. *Pay attention* to your body. Notice when your body is most relaxed, and follow through with the scenario that created the deep relaxation. In this way, you will make decisions that always result in success.

EXERCISE

Hold a five-pound weight (such as a sack of flour) in your outstretched hand. Keep your arm rigid like a board and hold the weight in your up-facing, open palm. Tell yourself: My arm is made of steel. The weight is a mere feather in my hand. I can hold this forever. I am strong. I am competent. I am magnificent.

Time yourself. How long can you hold the weight?

Wait a day. Do the same procedure again. This time, however, say negative things to yourself, such as: I am weak. I am a quitter. This weight is even heavier than it seems. I am a loser.

Time yourself.

You will see that there is a measurable difference between how you performed when you were thinking positive thoughts versus negative thoughts.

7
Smelling Foul Odors
Holding No Opinions

To see the universal and all pervading Spirit of Truth,
one must be able to love the meanest of creation as oneself.
–Mahatma Gandhi

Sengtsan, the third Chinese patriarch of Zen, is quoted as saying:

> *The Great Way is not difficult for those who have no preferences. When*
> *love and hate are both absent, everything becomes clear and undisguised.*
> *Make the smallest distinction, however, and heaven and earth are set infi-*
> *nitely apart. If you wish to see the truth, then hold no opinions for or*
> *against anything. To set up what you like against what you dislike is the*
> *disease of the mind. When the deep meaning of things is not understood,*
> *the mind's essential peace is disturbed to no avail.*

Reality is only what you make it. Ten people witnessing an accident will have ten different experiences of what is happening. Each is creating his or her experience with the programming in their ego. No one can say what is really happening, only what they perceive is happening.

Just because two people are in the same place at the same time doesn't mean that they are having the same experience. Remember Brittany and Abigail, the conjoined twins, who are obviously genetically identical. They have always been in the same place at the same time. However, their personalities are completely different because each of their bio-computers is being programmed with different information and this determines how their RAS constructs the filter system through which their egos experience life.

The twins will place importance on different ideas, will wind up having different memories, and will, therefore, have different ego structures. This results in each of them creating a different filter system and different realities in which they live. Even Brittany can't always know what her sister is experiencing.

YOU CREATE YOUR OWN REALITY

No one can ever presume to know another person's reality. I once had a tenant who removed an entire wall from the house he rented from me without ever consulting me. His intention was to install huge windows that he felt would enhance the view and add to the value of the house. When I confronted him with utter astonishment that he would do such a thing when it says in his lease he can't even paint a wall without permission, he seemed genuinely surprised. In that moment it became so very clear to me that I could in no way understand the reality in which this man lived!

What one person calls food, another might view as poison. What someone labels good, another may label as bad. Being judgmental is so much a part of us, few of us take the time to notice this function of the RAS.

GIVE YOUR FRIENDS A GIFT

Giving up your judgments is a genuine act of compassion for the people you interact with on a regular basis.

Consider the story of a boy who committed a crime. The boy's father was the local magistrate. Before sentencing, the boy's mother said to her husband, "Remember, he's our son." The father replied, "But I am the judge!"

Our linear, rational mind is locked into a dance with our ego and it can separate us from our heart. The heart is intuition, love, and compassion. When we judge others, we are letting our heads rule us rather than our hearts. The boy's mother is heart, i.e., compassion: Remember, he's our son. The father is head: But I am the judge! Judgment and compassion are opposites. To be compassionate, stop judging.

The heart brings us love, nurturing, peace, and spiritual clarity. The head brings us respect. Yet I know people who are respected, and at the same time, feared. If you are the type of person who would rather be loved than feared, stop judging.

LEMONS CAN BE TURNED INTO LEMONADE

In 1975, I was severely injured when a car struck me as I walked across a street. Years went by before I finally realized that my own feelings of self-pity, anger, and outrage were destroying any hope I had for peace of mind. Ultimately, I learned to stop judging my pain as the fault of another and stopped seeing myself as a victim.

By learning to use my injuries and pain as a focus upon which to meditate, I have grown to appreciate life in a way that would never have been possible if not for that accident. The accident has contributed to my being a more spiritual and compassionate person. Today, I can honestly say that it was the best thing that ever happened to me in terms of my spiritual growth.

Do you have a difficult situation that you've been forced to deal with in life? Have you been able to change your perceptions of it and use it as a springboard to growth?

Judgments, like the armor they become, limit your experience of life, insulating you from so much and making it difficult for you to ever appreciate another person's point of view. It separates you from others and makes the circle that comprises your life very, very small.

In *A Return to Love*, Marianne Williamson says:

> *Sometimes people think that calling on God means inviting a force into our lives that will make everything rosy. The truth is, it means inviting everything into our lives that will force us to grow—and growth can be messy. The purpose of life is to grow into our perfection. Once we call on God, everything that could anger us is on the way. Why? Because the place where we go into anger instead of love, is our wall. Any situation that pushes our buttons is a situation where we don't yet have the capacity to be unconditionally loving.*

MIND OVER MATTER

I've used many processes in my seminars to assist people in overcoming their anger and judgments, but the particularly extreme process described below works more effectively than any other.

Everyone sits in a circle. A challenge is offered: test the power of your mind to stop judging. With that, I pass a can of dog feces around the room. Whereas most people would normally be offended by this experience, in a setting where judgment is suspended, people use it as a spiritual exercise. The results are astonishing. People begin to savor the aroma in the can as if it were a lilac or a rose. They linger with the can and are slow to pass it on. As with the needle, some people use this opportunity of being without judgments to give themselves bliss.

A friend, Jana, goes to Peru every few years to study with a native shaman. On her last visit, the shaman told her and her group that he was going to conduct a sacred initiation.

The ceremony involved taking off all clothing and surrendering to the process at hand. A huge pit had been dug in the jungle. Several cartloads of animal dung were dumped into the pit. The shaman would take one person at a time and submerge them in the dung. More dung would be added, so that each person's body would be completely covered with the dung.

The shaman would then rub the dung into the person's mouth, push it into the ears, over the eyelids, and into the nose. This, of course, would all be performed in a highly ritualized, prayerful manner.

Participation was voluntary. Half the group opted not to participate. Jana was in the half that decided to go through the process. She had a tremendous amount of resistance to doing this, as I'm sure you can imagine!

It wasn't just initial resistance, Jana said; she resisted all the way through. Finally, when the dung was pushed into her mouth, she finally realized that she could choose her response. She could rebel. She could gag or vomit. Or she could give up all judgment, which, in fact, is what she did.

In the moment when it all seemed most unbearable, suddenly a switch was thrown and Jana had the experience of leaving her body. Time stood still. Colors swirled before her inner eye. She heard nothing. She smelled nothing. She tasted nothing. She had attained a bona fide altered state.

After an indeterminate time, the shaman plucked her from the pit and submerged her in the river. She regained awareness of her surroundings only after she had been submerged in the water. When she came up, her experience of being alive was transformed. Colors seemed more intense and brighter. The air seemed sweeter. And she had a deep sense of well-being that permeated every cell of her body.

As Jana left the river, she couldn't speak, because the power of her realization overwhelmed her.

The next morning, when the entire group reunited for breakfast, Jana noticed that the people who did not participate were chitchatting idly; but the people who had participated in the ritual were speechless, grinning broadly, glowing with a beatific aura. She said it would have been impossible to communicate exactly what the process had done to them with those who hadn't participated; but it seemed quite apparent to those involved in the idle chatter that their comrades had undergone something profound.

People who are judgmental tend to be narrow-minded and neurotic. They limit what they are willing to experience and thus stifle their education and development. Many people who claim to be on a spiritual path, who meditate and do yoga, still exhibit neuroses and fail to realize that their own judgmental nature is to blame.

When you are uptight or being petty, you are experiencing a by-product of being a judgmental person. When you are uncomfortable around people, your judgments are the cause of your discomfort. When new situations make you tense, they are showing you that your own judgments are interfering with your ability to be spontaneous and joyful all the time.

The world is like a mirror. It shows you where your judgments lie every time you are willing to pay attention to your dis-ease. Instead of running away from what you usually term as unpleasant situations, you can learn to seek them out as opportunities to work on yourself and become free of your judgments and the limitation that they cause in your life.

True love means to be unconditionally accepting. Discrimination and bigotry are the opposites of love; they are the children of our judgments. In the following exercise, you can use the people that you judge as if they are your teachers.

EXERCISE

Think of someone you know well and dislike. Put his or her name on the top of a blank sheet of paper. On the paper, make a list of all the things you dislike—using his or her name in each case—about this person.

When the list is complete, cross out the name at the top of the paper and put your own name there instead. For each item on the list, substitute your name for the person's whom you dislike. Instead of, "I dislike

Joe because he's such a failure," it now reads, "I dislike myself when I fail." By doing this, Joe becomes a mirror that enables you to see your judgments; not just about others, but about yourself as well.

Even if you aren't ready to give up your judgments, at least notice that they cause a certain degree of narrow-mindedness and color your experience of life.

8
Snapping Pointed Arrows with Your Throat
Pushing past Paradox

To see the world in a grain of sand,
And heaven in a wildflower;
Hold infinity in your hand,
And eternity in an hour.
—William Blake

Personal growth is similar to peeling layers off an onion. Every time one complete layer is removed, another one is revealed. People are sometimes surprised to discover this characteristic of the growth process. Generally, we'd prefer to believe that at some point we're going to be finished. The truth is, however, the process of realizing your full potential is never complete. If you are still alive, you can grow.

After you successfully complete some of the challenges posed by *Extreme Spirituality*, you'll find that much of what you used to believe was impossible is now not only possible, but easy. Remember Virginia? Before she did it, she would have said it was impossible for her to break a brick with her hand. Maybe others, but not her. Jenny, too, discovered that when she finally stepped up to the task, she broke the board easily.

Each of them had her RAS reprogrammed that day. Their new programming: all is possible.

Are there things you would like to accomplish but have been unwilling to consider because you've always thought they would be impossible? If so, begin changing that pattern by acknowledging that all things are possible when you are connected to a higher power. When you feel inseparably connected to the source of all creation, at all times, then all things are indeed possible!

Jesus referred to his miracles and said: *All that I have done, you too shall be able to do. And even far greater things than these.*

I have always encouraged people to take those words literally.

In exploring how to teach others to make the impossible possible, I learned of a practice attributed to Native Americans. It is said that some among them would place the pointed end of an arrow into their throats, and, with the feathered end firmly lodged against a tree, they would push into the arrow with all their strength. Instead of being impaled and suffering an agonizing death, the arrow would snap! *Extreme* spirituality!

It sounds miraculous. And, although physical laws can explain what makes the arrow break—the trachea can tolerate more force than the arrow can before it snaps; the metal tip is sharp but not that sharp—explanations don't affect the absolute awe that overwhelms you the first time you do something that you had always perceived as impossible.

The first time I placed the arrow at my throat, so that the metal point poked coldly into the soft V just beneath my Adam's apple, it was easy for me to witness the voices in my head. They were screaming, "Impossible! Impossible!"

I told my intellectual mind that if it was possible for anyone else to do this, then it was also possible for me. I gave myself an inner pep talk and told myself that God had not brought me this far along the path only to kill me now. But as I began to push, instead of feeling the arrow yield or bend in any way, I felt a stabbing discomfort, not quite yet pain, and I began to think, "Oh no. What's happening?" My rational mind was taking over, and I instinctively eased back from the tip of the arrow.

I began the process of paying attention to the voices inside my head and saw all the classic phrases that began with "Oh no ...," "What if ...," or "I can't . . ." I shouted out loud, "Shut up!" and I pushed again. There was a split second of pain, but I was trained by the fire and the needle, so I recognized it as the pain associated with mere sunburn rather than charred stumps. Instantly, my RAS shut down the old "Oh no!" program and my bio-computer ran the new command: "Oh yes! This is what I've trained for. This is my opportunity!"

By changing my mind, I also changed my body's actions, and I was able to push through ego-resistance and ultimately snap the arrow. The moment was an ecstatic experience of extreme spirituality.

You know that positive thinkers literally live in a different chemical environment than negative thinkers. Your attitudes, in part, determine the strength of your body, the effectiveness of your immune system, and ultimately, the state of your health and whether or not you'll recover from a major disease. This is not a philosophical or abstract concept: it is a hard fact!

DEALING WITH PARADOX

Whenever you test your strength and spirit in an effort to grow, there comes a moment when Princess Paradox stands stark naked in front of you. The steel point on the arrow is sharp. It hurts to push against it. But you know you can't ease up if you want to grow. And the more you push, the sharper the pain.

So here you are: one voice within your head is saying "Ouch!" "Ouch!" and another voice is saying, "Push!" "Push!" "Push harder!"

"Ouch!" versus "Keep pushing!"

As you make your final thrust forward, you are not only pushing the physical arrow into one of the softest, most delicate parts of your body, you are also pushing beyond the limitations posed by every paradox.

Our minds are not wired to deal with paradox. But the epiphany that accompanies these kinds of acts of self-growth instantly produces a significant degree of permanent, indelible, lifetime empowerment. The electrochemical surge it causes in the brain and body becomes programming that the RAS never forgets. Your brain has been rewired.

LUCY AND HER ARROW

At a seminar in an Atlantic City casino, everyone in the group, except Lucy, was able to break an arrow. Lucy called to the group, "Help me. I need you. Help me do this thing." People called back, "You can do it, Lucy. We're with you!" Still, she could not bring herself to push with 100 percent of her will and 100 percent of her strength.

Since the purpose of the seminar was not simply to break arrows but for self-examination, Lucy, my brother, Barry, and I left the meeting room and entered the casino, where we would explore, using the slot machines as biofeedback devices, what was really holding Lucy back. Before we had even approached a slot machine, Barry pointed out to

Lucy that she was like Dorothy in *The Wizard of Oz*, always looking for someone else to take her home, when the whole time she had the power herself. She was wearing the ruby slippers.

Something clicked with Lucy. With Barry's words, she saw that whenever she was tested, she would say to herself, "I can't do this alone." She not only saw how her RAS was using negative programming, she consciously changed it on the spot. She shut down the "I can't" and screamed, "Yes! Yes! Yes! Yes!" In fact, Lucy just about jumped in the air and clicked her heels. When you change your programming, it instantly changes the way you feel; yes, you can actually feel it!

Lucy ran up to a slot machine and said, "Barry, watch this." She pulled the handle and hit the $2,500 jackpot. She ran back to the seminar room before the rest of the group returned and snapped the arrow.

I am a skeptic by nature and did not believe in miracles, and so I was blind to them and never experienced them. After realizing that nothing is impossible with God and observing ordinary people accomplishing unbelievable victories in my workshops, I now experience and witness miracles all the time.

EXERCISE

Have you ever been told that something was impossible, and yet you did it? Recall the feelings of triumph and the amount of energy it liberated in you. Is that a feeling you would like to experience again? Assuming that you do indeed want to have that in your life again, create a goal for yourself, one that would require you to strrrrretch. For example, instead of hiring a contractor, tackle a home-improvement project by yourself.

Instead of taking the usual three months to complete a task at work, resolve to do it in half the time. Instead of running from an unsatisfactory marriage, create a plan to make the marriage work.

List all the internal voices that tell you your goal is impossible. For example: I can't do this because I only have one leg. Or, I can't stay in this marriage because my partner doesn't appreciate me. Or, I can't complete this project because I don't have the needed skills.

Now create a new list and take each line from the first list and alter it like so:

"I only have one leg but I can do this," "I lack the skills I need, but I can learn them," and so on.

Every time you do something that you thought you could not do, it changes your image of yourself. Soon, instead of seeing yourself as a loser because your personal history has always depicted you that way, you will start thinking of yourself as a winner because you have given yourself a new personal history. Helen Keller wasn't a great person because she overcame being deaf and blind; she was who she was *because* she was deaf and blind. The paradox lies in the fact that she took a seeming weakness and used it for strength.

9
Aiming for Excellence
Using Your Work as a Spiritual Path

Greatness is determined by service.
–Martin Luther King, Jr.

OUTER WORK REFLECTS THE INNER WORKINGS

Just as a computer is separate from the software that runs it, you're not your programming.

Remember GIGO—garbage in, garbage out? A truly excellent computer can work badly if it operates with crummy programming. You too may be an excellent human being, but because of crummy programming, you are not getting what you want; or are getting a lot of what you don't want.

Going to work can be an exercise in extreme spirituality for anyone who wants to aim for excellence and perfection. Haven't you always longed for a job that filled you with such satisfaction that you couldn't wait to get to work? You don't need to change jobs to have this experience right now. That is the beauty of practicing extreme spirituality. You can be the change you want, starting right now. Extreme spirituality means that you can proceed from exactly where you are this very minute.

A man who loved running a market bought some land and built a very respectable supermarket. He was a man who not only followed his religion, he lived it. His employees loved him and he loved them. It was a pleasure to shop in his market. The people who worked there seemed upbeat and happy. The market was a well-designed machine being run with excellent programming.

Eventually, the man sold his store and retired. Many of the same employees continued to work there, but their morale nose-dived. The new owner was not attentive to his employees or to details. A shopping trip there became fraught with rudeness and inaccuracies. A once-excellent machine was being run by crummy programming. Business rapidly declined.

How could a "tune-up" help this situation? Isn't it possible to inject this market with a spiritual transfusion? The challenge of transforming this market can be made easy by creating it as a spiritual game in which every player wins.

Since most of the employees are church-going Christians, it would be relatively simple to align the entire process with basic Christian tenets. Jesus said, *"Seek first the kingdom of heaven, and all else will be added to you."*

YOUR JOB CAN BE HEAVEN

The kingdom to which Jesus referred is not a physical place, like Albuquerque. It is a state of being. It is the process of attaining and experiencing perfection. *"The kingdom of heaven lies within,"* said Jesus.

This great teacher also asked that we return his affection by doing good to others as if we were doing good to him. To walk this path with perfection is to arrive at the kingdom. The kingdom, of course, is the spiritual destination that we are seeking. It is the end of suffering. It is why we practice extreme spirituality.

If extreme spirituality directs us to make our work a spiritual practice, each day becomes an opportunity to grow. Therefore, in the example of the grocery store, a butcher could carve every steak as if he was carving it for his spiritual master. He could serve each customer as if he is serving his Lord. In this way, his job itself becomes an act of worship.

The benefits for the butcher are obvious. The benefits for the market are manifold. As an employer, now you have happy employees. You also have happy customers, because everyone appreciates service. You also have more profit, because there is no carelessness, and far less loss.

PERFECTION IS A SPIRITUAL EXPERIENCE

Everyone on a team should aim for excellence, be they a cashier, bagger, stocker, baker, or produce clerk. The idea is to make the market itself an object of worship, knowing that the market—just like the arrow, the fire, or the brick—is a metaphor for being able to express your devotion to a higher power.

The process is actually very enjoyable, and when you are not enjoying it, there is a marvelous opportunity to use the situation as a way to learn something. So now there are no longer "problems" in your life, only opportunities and lessons.

If you are a manager, you have a chance to upgrade an entire cadre of people to a new level of happiness and fulfillment. If you are self-employed, you too have a chance to practice perfection. Let your work be an expression of your own uniqueness and a reflection of your values.

HATS OFF TO HYATT

I once conducted a corporate firewalking seminar at the Hyatt Regency Hotel in Greenwich, Connecticut. As soon as I entered the lobby I knew there was something unusual about the place. There was an obvious joy circulating around the room. The employees seemed ecstatic about something, and patrons were infected by the spirit that seemed to float in the air. It was hard to imagine that anyone could feel anything but "up" in this environment.

Over the next two days, I noticed that my every request was answered as if I were Bill Gates, and the person serving me seemed as if he just couldn't do enough for me. Tasks were done promptly and perfectly every time. Not only the employees but the entire building was a temple of excellence: the linen and table service, the housekeeping, the bars; every minute detail shone with excellence.

When I went to speak with a maintenance engineer about shovels and rakes, I saw that the walls of his department were covered with positive affirmations that encouraged him to aim for excellence. He said that the morale could be attributed to the vision of one man: his general manager, who had a way of making every single employee feel important. Every person on the team knew that it would not be the same without him or her.

Imagine what your daily life would be like if you regularly encountered service and attitudes like those at the Hyatt in Greenwich? What if this kind of service was the rule wherever you went, and not the exception to it? We have become so used to poor service and mediocrity that when an exception occurs, we notice it as we would an apple growing on an orange tree. If you are in a position to bring about positive changes in your work environment, don't wait. Do it now.

HOW WOULD YOU DEFINE EXCELLENCE?

You may feel that your circumstances don't resemble the situation at the Hyatt. Then create your own situation wherein you can aim for excellence as a way of walking the path of extreme spirituality.

Only you know what excellence is for you. You are not required to measure yourself against any standard but your own. For example, I make primitive rattles as a form of folk art. I stretch leather over gourds and attach the gourds to sticks, which I then decorate with fur, feathers, and beads.

My first few rattles were greatly admired. The admirers didn't notice the little snotlike balls of glue and rubber cement that clung to some of the feathers and beads. Even when they congratulated me, I knew inside myself that I could do better, because I had an inner vision of what the perfect rattle would look like. Fifteen rattles later, I made my first rattle that I looked at and considered to be absolutely excellent, by my standard.

Getting there required me to walk a path that was guided by my own inner vision. As I aimed for excellence and the perfect rattle, that part of my life became a living meditation.

Play this like a game, not as if it were a chore to get done. Remember, life is not a problem to be solved (crummy programming); it's a spiritual adventure to be enjoyed (excellent programming).

EXERCISE

Set yourself a task and resolve beforehand to perform it as an exercise in extreme spirituality. It could be something simple like baking a cake or something monumental like organizing a charity ball. As you undertake the activity, remember to approach every facet of the project as an act of worship or devotion, an opportunity to create and experience perfection. Use affirmation cards like "Let it be easy!" or any other strategy that will keep your intention foremost in your mind. You can post pictures on the wall that motivate you, play music that inspires you, or recruit another person with whom to share the task. When you are able to win with this exercise in some area of your life other than your job, you can transfer the lessons learned to your daily job and transform your work into a spiritual practice. In May, 1999, *US News & World Report* featured a story on corporate training techniques and noted that spirituality-based training techniques proved to measurably improve productivity and profits.

10
Sweating
Finding Joy in Vulnerability

Sweet, sweet surrender. Live, live without fear.
–John Denver

I once had a spiritual teacher who shone a flashlight on the wall, commenting on what a bright, strong light it created. She then took Windex and a tissue, cleaned the lens, and commented on how much brighter the light now seemed.

The Native Americans have long known the value of cleaning your light. A spiritual sweat lodge ceremony is like Windex and tissue, cleaning our lens so that our light shines brighter. It is a perfect exercise for extreme spirituality.

For some of my longer seminars, I construct a Native American sweat lodge. The sweat lodge is constructed by bending willow branches into a snug, igloolike shape. This dome is then covered with black plastic and insulated with blankets and quilts. A large fire is lit outside the lodge and rocks are heated in the fire until they are glowing, red-hot. The glowing stones are then carried to an earthen pit dug in the center of the sweat lodge. When the door flap is thrown closed, the glowing stones are sprayed with water. The steam heats the sweat lodge to temperatures well over 150 degrees Fahrenheit.

Men and women sit together naked in a tight circle around the central pit. Each occupant of the lodge has about twelve inches of space in which to sit, so the experience is one of being hunched together like sardines in a small can. No one can see anyone else, as it is pitch black.

The purpose is spiritual growth.

Within the lodge one person leads the ceremony. Each person gets a turn to offer a prayer or to simply speak from his heart. On one level, this is just a group of people sitting in a circle, praying aloud. Yet, on another, everyone is coping with the extremely challenging physical circumstances. It is uncomfortable to sit hunched so tightly with so many people. It is an effort to breathe the hot, steam-filled air. It is a feat not to pass out altogether. The space is so tight, the sweat so universal, that it is hardly possible to determine where your body ends and where the next person begins.

As people begin to pray out loud, they often burst into tears as a result of feeling so vulnerable. In that moment, the ego lets down its guard and people get to experience a genuine spiritual reality, untainted by perceptions usually controlled by the RAS. Afterward, participants frequently express that they felt a direct experience of God in that instant. All that was required was for the ego to die for a split second.

The sweat lodge is a metaphor for whatever situation requires us to surrender. Of course, what gets surrendered is the ego: rigidity, resistance, judgment, arrogance, defensiveness, hostility—the small you.

You don't have to join a sweatlodge experience to benefit from its lessons. You can re-create the experience by consciously placing yourself in situations in which you are vulnerable, uncomfortable, and required to grow.

WHO ARE YOU?

The spiritual practices in this book are not about being physically tough; they're about being spiritually tough. When you make the decision to sweat through it, you are empowered to push through ego-resistance when it tries to persuade you to give up and be less than you can be. "When the going gets tough, the tough get going" means that people of spiritual conviction walk the path even when challenges appear. These are the people whose brand of extreme spirituality has prepared them for all eventualities. This is who I hope you are becoming.

People's behavior in the sweat lodge is generally a perfect microcosm of how they behave in life. If people want to get out as soon as the temperature begins to rise, you can be fairly sure that this is the way that person behaves in life when stress levels go up. I encourage people to pay attention to their patterns while in the sweat lodge and, when they encounter a pattern that predictably limits them and rips them off, to risk breaking that pattern once and for all. The risk is always to the ego. The best way to deal with the ego inside the sweat lodge is to tell it: Today is a good day to die.

And the best way to deal with the ego *outside* the sweat lodge is to tell it: Today is a good day to die.

Before I learned how to sweat through my ego, it always stopped me just before I had accomplished my goal. I would be the quitter on any team. I would give in or I would give up; rarely would I see a difficult project through to a conclusion. Now, once I make the decision to see something through to completion, I never give up. I'd rather die! It's not always easy, but it's always worth it. And who dies? Only my small self with the big ego.

You can instantly begin making positive changes in your life by looking at some of your unfinished projects. If you quit prematurely, perhaps you now have enough resolve to go back and complete some of the tasks you left undone for whatever reason you thought was valid at the time. Even if you aren't ready to see something all the way through to completion, do something that will at least move the project forward. Sometimes, by the yard a task can be hard, but by the inch, it's a cinch.

EXERCISE

I once went to a Japanese spa. The hot pool was very hot and the cold pool was very cold. The cold water seemed more challenging, and few people lingered there. Yet one old Japanese man spent almost a half hour sitting in the cold water with his eyes closed. Inspired by his example, I slid into the water and discovered that resisting the chill seemed to make it colder. But by using the techniques learned in the sweat lodge, I surrendered to the cold and soon was experiencing genuine joy.

Try this at home in your own bathtub. Create a tub of very hot water one day and a tub of very cold water on another day. Practice surrendering until you attain real joy from the experience.

11
Walking Barefoot on Shards of Broken Glass
Creating Conscious Moments

Be here now.
–Ram Dass

A Sufi tale tells of a man who was terrified of snakes. One day, while at a mountain resort, someone casually said, "Be careful of the poisonous snakes we have around here." This completely ruined the man's day. Every time he passed a shadow, his body contracted. His head was constantly turning, looking for snakes. Finally, that night, when the man entered his darkened room, while fumbling for the light switch, he saw on the floor a coiled snake ready to strike. He became so overwhelmed by fear that he had a heart attack and dropped dead.

The next morning, the housekeeper found the man lying dead on the floor next to a coil of rope.

What killed this man? Certainly it wasn't a snake, for there was no snake. What killed him was false evidence appearing real: F.E.A.R. Our fears are always turning ropes into snakes.

This Sufi tale illustrates how the RAS constantly shows us what we think is happening rather than allowing us to experience what is really going on. For this reason, it is important to pay attention to our fears rather than avoid situations that trigger them, and many of the exercises in my seminars facilitate this.

Recall the story of the monk, the tigers, and the strawberry from chapter 2. There was a specific moment when the monk put the strawberry in his mouth, and he paid attention to it 100 percent. When we pay attention in this way, something amazing occurs. In order to be 100 percent committed, no portion of our mind can be wandering; we can't be thinking about something in the future or something from the past. We can't be comparing the present with any other experience, since the process of consideration would cause the mind to again wander and would dilute the 100 percent. When you master paying attention in this way, eventually no part of you is watching yourself; no part of you is even aware that you are having an experience. Because you have *become* the experience.

When you taste a strawberry with 100 percent attentive awareness, your experience is that you have *become* the strawberry. When you smell a rose and pay attention 100 percent, your experience is that you have *become* the smell of the rose. You literally merge with what you experience and go beyond even being the experiencer.

These conscious moments instantly bring us into the here and now. It is precisely this experience that meditation produces. It is important to recognize and label these conscious moments when they occur so that we have a frame of reference and know what it is we are aiming for in our meditations.

LIVING IN THE MOMENT

Certain situations can assist in putting us in this conscious mode. The practices in this book facilitate attaining these conscious moments. Many sports also produce these conscious moments. Downhill skiers are forced, by the quickly changing scenario, to stay in the here and now. Skiing is a great meditation!

You can make a decision to seek these conscious moments in any day-to-day circumstances. A butcher can trim meat as a meditation, a road-worker can fill potholes as a meditation, a painter can paint houses as a meditation. It is simply a matter of being 100 percent attentive in the present moment. Many times we are unconscious as we move through our days. We need to be reminded how far away from a conscious moment we have drifted. If you step in shit—literally or figuratively—don't gripe. Be grateful for the wake-up call to consciousness.

For it is in these conscious moments that we receive the insights that broaden our understanding and add to the depth of our knowledge. After enough of these have accumulated, we start to realize spiritually things that had earlier been merely understood intellectually. In his book *Where Did I Come From?* Peter Mayle explains the reproductive process for children. He attempts describing an orgasm by saying it is similar to a tickling sensation followed by a big sneeze. Thus, kids may grow up with an intellectual idea of what an orgasm feels like, but it isn't until they mature and actually have the experience themselves that understanding becomes realization.

These realizations lead to true wisdom from which the paradoxical nature of the universe is clearly perceived. Those who live in this special place are referred to as holy men, medicine women, shamans, or saints.

Extreme spirituality doesn't suggest that everyone live there, for that would make raising a family quite a distraction; but rather, that we check in from time to time so that we can maintain perspective and harmony as we go through our daily routines.

GLASS WALKING AS MEDITATION

Walking on shards of broken glass is an extreme way of arriving at this place, and I use it as an exercise in some of my seminars to bring people into the here and now. I have a crate filled with fifty pounds of broken glass. I used a hammer and smashed goblets, pickle jars, wine bottles, glass candleholders, etc.

I rake the shards into a runway, demonstrate how to walk across it, and then invite people to walk barefoot across the broken glass themselves. Of course, like all other challenges in my seminars, participation is completely voluntary. These kinds of approaches toward extreme spirituality have nothing to do with courage. There is no pressure, and in fact, it is acknowledged that it takes more courage to say "No, this is not for me, not today," especially if all your friends actually have done it before you.

Of the thousand people I have led over six-foot beds of broken glass, not one has cut their feet. The way to walk across shards of broken glass is exactly the opposite way one walks across hot coals. The glass demands slow, conscious moments of extreme attentiveness, just like the boy with the bowl of water on his head. No one quickly bounds onto shards of glass. The task demands attention. People never forget that it is razor-sharp glass underneath their feet. They need no other incentive to pay attention! They are not *learning* to pay attention, they are just doing it. And hence, they are not learning meditation, they are actually practicing it as they walk across the glass.

The glass becomes the teacher. Because there isn't another ego involved in the confrontation, the impersonal nature of the event makes it easier for you to set your own ego aside and receive insights at a much more profound level.

By putting your attention on your feet, you can know when each foot is being equally supported by all the points and edges. It is a conscious moment.

These conscious moments act as neutralizers for a stress-filled world. An entire day of stress can be neutralized with just a few minutes of meditation. It's like the well-advertised antacid that absorbs many times its own weight.

EXERCISE

Fill a bowl with popcorn. Arbitrarily pluck one of the popped kernels from the bowl. Study it with 100 percent of your attention. Put it back in the bowl and gently mix the bowl. Now find the piece of popcorn you studied earlier.

The process of focusing on the originally selected piece of popcorn is a conscious moment. It is a meditation. Learn to recognize that state and find ways to include meditation in your daily life.

12
Healing Your Body
Applying the Secret of Spontaneous Remissions

God alone is Real and the goal of life is to become united with
God through love.
–Meher Baba

Extreme spirituality implies radical approaches toward almost everything in our lives, including our health and healing. If faith healing, accelerated healing, and radiant, vibrant health are available to anyone at all on the planet, then they can be available to you. If spontaneous remissions of disease occur even occasionally, the implication is that it can occur for you too.

I was once eating a bowl of ice cream, and because I wasn't paying attention, I dropped the bowl. It smashed on the floor, spreading broken glass in every direction. I spent a few minutes cleaning the floor and, since it seemed that no glass had gotten into the ice cream, I put the ice cream into a new bowl. After eating a few spoonfuls, I suddenly thought a sliver of glass had lodged in the back of my throat.

In truth, there was no glass in the ice cream, but I did not know that at the time. Because I imagined that there was actually glass stuck in my throat, my blood pressure went up, my heart rate accelerated, I began to perspire, and I exhibited physical symptoms that mirrored what would actually have happened if, in fact, there really was a piece of glass in my throat. My mind was causing changes in my body.

When we look at ourselves holistically, we see that our physical state is a by-product of this mind-body connection. As we've seen, when the chemistry of the brain changes, it affects the chemistry of the body. When the chemistry of the body changes, it affects the chemistry of the brain. That is why eating junk food can cause depression.

LOVE AND LAUGHTER CAN HEAL YOU

This mind-body connection reveals new ways to take conscious control of our immune systems and our healing systems. We can actually create states of mind that contribute to the optimal level of functioning in all our bodily systems.

For example, we know that laughter causes the thymus gland to become engorged with blood, to enlarge and function better, and depression causes it to shrink and become sluggish. The thymus gland produces T-cells as part of its immune function. Therefore, a person fighting cancer would be wise to monitor his or her state of mind as much as possible. Humor and a positive outlook can influence the course of recovery. Anything that we can do to relieve stress and encourage physical relaxation will enhance our health and physical well-being. Positive decisions create the electrochemical changes that reprogram the RAS in ways that contribute to resourceful physical states. Positive thinkers live in a different chemical environment than negative thinkers.

Thoughts, attitudes, and outlook will often, although not always, mean the difference between recovery and survival, or death.

One of the cornerstones in the Christian religion is faith healing. It was part and parcel of the ministry of Jesus. He goes so far as to say: You will place your hands on the sick, and they will get well. This kind of reality is perfectly aligned with the concepts of extreme spirituality. It offers us possibilities that previously seemed fanciful. Those who practice it, or walk their talk, are the examples of extreme spirituality that are needed for inspiration. People of primitive cultures, including the Native Americans, also practiced spiritual healing, although they never labeled it as such. Usually the shaman or medicine man was simply viewed as having special powers to cause these kinds of healing. Conversely, they were also seen as having the power to curse and cast evil spells that could harm or kill. Dr. Walter Cannon, the famed American medical researcher, wrote about this and how the power of suggestion, in the hands of a doctor, not only can heal disease, but if not properly employed, cause disease as well. Dr. Cannon concluded that when a person is certain they are about to die, their acceptance of that certainty causes them to "keep their appointment with death."

The condition of a person's immune system can be determined with medical tests. Researchers can evaluate immune function based on the presence or absence of certain substances in blood, urine, tissue, or saliva. In one study, David McClelland, a psychologist working at the Harvard University Health Center, measured the Immunoglobulin A levels in a group of volunteers. The Immunoglobulin A antibody is instrumental in fighting colds and flu. The group was then shown a movie about Mother Teresa and her life's charitable work with orphans in Calcutta. After the movie, Immunoglobulin A levels were again measured and were found to have increased. Researchers dubbed this immuno-enhancement as the Mother Teresa Effect, whereby even being in the presence of love can have a biochemical impact on the physical body. We can heal with, and be healed by, love.

No longer is healing without conventional medicine considered to be on the fringe. Dr. Howard Hall, a psychologist at Penn State University, did a white blood cell count on a group of subjects. He then taught them how to use their minds to visualize the white blood cells multiplying and attacking cancer cells. Afterward, he again took blood samples and discovered that white blood cell counts had increased anywhere from 10 to 25 percent. Mainstream medical doctors are all aware of the breakthroughs in cancer therapy using this knowledge. Medical doctors such as Andrew Weil, Bernie Siegel, Carl Simonton, and Deepak Chopra have documented incredible results using an approach suggested by extreme spirituality. In fact, Weil reports that tumors the size of grapefruits have gone into complete remission, sometimes in only a matter of days.

Dr. Siegel frequently relates the story about a patient who was told that she only had a short time to live. She went home, put her affairs in order, and waited to die. For the first time in her life, she enjoyed total peace of mind. That peace of mind, however, proved to be just what her ailing immune system needed, and the woman lived on for many more years.

Dr. Weil tells of a patient who turned to God for the first time once she found out that she was only a few months from death. Her spiritual conversion so transformed her normally bitter personality that a spontaneous remission occurred. A metaphoric knot was untied so that it no longer was constricting the woman's immune system.

Before I understood the mind-body connection and how I could take conscious control of my physical body, I was always suffering from poor health. I used to get a cold or flu about six times a year. In 1987 I finally made a conscious decision to change my level of health. I reprogrammed my bio-computer in 1987, and for the past fourteen years, I have not had one single cold or flu at all.

Amazing stories about health and healing abound. Spontaneous remission of cancer is no longer hearsay. If you or a loved one is suffering from cancer, you have access through the Internet to support groups, and in bookstores, to information documenting the link between positive mental attitude and recovery. Of course it is true that when it's our time to die, nothing will prevent death, not mental imagery, drugs, or surgery. However, a positive mental attitude can greatly enhance the quality of someone's life while they have it, even if death is inevitable.

You can find evidence of people who were told they'd never walk again, and today they run marathons. You can read about people who were once blind and now they see. People who were given only weeks to live are today enjoying healthy lives years after they were supposed to succumb. So why not employ positive thinking and see what happens?

If we label these incidents miraculous, it places them beyond the realm of an expected, everyday occurrence. We need to start seeing this as our birthright: a paradigm of health and healing.

Norman Cousins, in his famous book *Anatomy of an Illness*, describes how he used laughter and positive thinking to overcome his own terminal illness. After his recovery, he was invited to participate in a study at the Harvard University Medical School. Researchers were trying to determine the chemistry of laughter. That study eventually demonstrated that substances known as neuropeptides are released in response to our thoughts. These neuropeptides then combine and recombine in so many ways that we can literally manufacture within ourselves any substance that can be found in a pharmacy. Endorphins are examples of this. We literally manufacture these morphinelike substances in our own bodies and they are as effective at blocking pain as synthetic medications. Endorphins also make you feel good.

NO SIDE EFFECTS

As a result, we can now learn techniques for healing ourselves and blocking pain without using drugs. And of course the nice part of this approach is that drug-related side effects are no longer an issue.

Now that you have this information, why wait until you are ill or infirm to put it to use? You can construct a new paradigm this very minute. You can dedicate your life to the extreme spiritual practice of living love. You can infuse every cell of your body with love and visualize each nerve and fiber working easily together in perfect harmony. All you need to do to see it, is to be it. Health and healing are your birthright!

EXERCISE

The Church of Christian Science maintains an archive of certifiable health reversals that can be linked to a change of heart or mind. Love and positive thinking can clearly be curative. Pettiness, mean-spiritedness, anger, and hate clearly cause ulcers, high blood pressure, and all kinds of other woes.

Eastern religion views the human body as a temple in which the living spirit resides. Do you treat your body like a temple?

Make a decision to do three things to improve your health. It can be a decision to start a fitness program or to make a change in diet, but only commit to something that you know you will be able to do. If you are going to start a weight-loss program, be realistic in what you attempt so that you can avoid getting discouraged and not following through with your good intentions.

Use the tools of positive thinking and extreme spirituality to assist you in giving up smoking, drinking less alcohol, and avoiding overworking. Use the tools to create a lifestyle that includes meditation, service, love, and play.

After attaining the three goals you pursued to improve your health, constantly create new goals and make new decisions until you are completely satisfied with your own level of health and vitality.

13
Fasting
Housecleaning for Spirit

*Most Eastern philosophers and super-yogis, known for
their long life, mental efficiency and spiritual awareness,
fast regularly, along with their meditation, to attain
long life and a high level of spirituality.*
–Paava Airola

UNCLOGGING THE BODY FOR SPIRITUAL CLARITY

Like sweating, fasting is a way of cleansing your body. Many would say this
is too extreme, especially those who are addicted to food. However, the
way I practice fasting is extremely easy.

Sometimes I drink carrot juice. Other times, I boil fresh vegetables
to extract their nutrients, and then drink the broth. I also boil potatoes,
rice, or oats and drink the water to get carbohydrates. I make lemonade
using whole lemons and pure maple syrup, not only to create a source of
calories, but also because it tastes good.

It is so easy, that I often forget I am fasting. My longest fast was forty
days, but every year I routinely fast for five, seven, or ten days at a time. No,

I am not anorexic. I simply have discovered a way to fast that eliminates experiencing hunger, and markedly increases spiritual clarity. A forty-day fast isn't that long; people have fasted for over two hundred days.

Fasting, of course, if undertaken for the wrong reasons, or handled incorrectly, can injure your health. As with every spiritual practice in this book, I am not suggesting you need to actually do what is described in these pages. It is more important for you to extract the essential teaching or insights that people receive from participating in these extreme processes. Once you comprehend where it is that these exercises take people, you can get there any way that works for you. You might wish to try some of the methods from the book, try none at all, or devise your own methods to assist you in experiencing the states to which extreme spirituality can take you.

FASTING CAN CAUSE ALTERED STATES

Fasting is an age-old tradition for restoring health and vigor that in recent years has found scientific support for its benefits. In 1973, I began fasting as a way to restore health, but was soon amazed at how well it restored spiritual clarity as well, especially at a time when my ego had actually fooled me into thinking I was already very clear.

Those who live to eat, rather than eat to live, will view people who fast as akin to the man who kept hitting himself on the head simply because it felt so good when he stopped! While it is true that you will appreciate and savor the taste of food far more after a long fast, that is not the reason to do it.

When we fast, we deprive the body of many things, including fat and protein. This stimulates a process known as autolysis, a sanitized word for eating oneself. The body begins to digest cells contained in various parts of the body. It begins with the damaged cells, toxic deposits, and fat. As a result, while fasting, we eliminate accumulated debris that clogs our systems. We lose a bit of weight and are cleansed. As a result, we look better, feel better, can expect more years in our lives and more life in our years.

If you are going to do a fast lasting more than one day, be sure to cleanse your colon with a daily enema or by using powdered psyllium seed husks or a commercial product that creates a bowel movement by forcing some bulk into your intestine.

In addition to every other benefit produced by fasting, it often precipitates an altered state, described so perfectly by my brother, Barry:

> All of a sudden I would be someplace else! Not asleep, definitely nothing like sleep. No visions either. It was a space beyond sleep, visions, thoughts, or words. People who define their existence through thoughts and feelings will not be able to relate to this.
>
> When I came out, my thoughts naturally returned. The only way that I knew that I just came from a special place was by how I felt when I returned to the conscious world.
>
> I literally felt transformed. Joy and peace radiated through me. Not the simple kind of happiness that comes from being in a good mood, but something much deeper. It was the bliss that can only come from the knowledge that everything is perfect. That everything is God. That I am God. That there is no need to strive, only to be aware.

There are many books available on fasting. One of my favorites is *Are You Confused?* by Paavo Airola. He introduces the idea that juice and broth can simply be viewed as liquid meals. As a result, you do not feel like you are depriving yourself, and I have found this approach to be both effort-less and fun.

I recommend fasting only one day at a time. Even when I've fasted for weeks, I am really fasting one day at a time. Each morning I make the decision to fast for that day. I don't start out a fast by defining it in advance as a two-day or a four-day fast . . . it's always just for one day.

When I first began including fasting as part of my approach to extreme spirituality, I fasted one day each week. I'd call that day GURU Day, for "Gee, you are you!" This reminded me that my best teacher is an inner teacher. I'd drink a lot of juice throughout the day. There was absolutely no hunger involved. Unless you have a medical condition that would prohibit fasting, and if you are healthy, you can do a one-day fast, once a week. Of course, before you fast, talk with your health-care provider.

CREATE A SPECIAL DAY FOR YOURSELF

I know many people create mental images of fasting that have absolutely nothing to do with the actual experience itself. Initially, mental images of firewalking, skydiving, or shards of glass also conjure up horrible pic-tures that imply danger, injury, discomfort, or pain. And yet, the path of extreme spirituality employs each of those very modalities as vehicles for personal growth. People not only *don't* have negative experiences of these practices, they extol them!

I really do love to eat, so the only bad thing I can say about a longer fast is that it sometimes gets a little boring. Images of ice cream sundaes sometimes test my resolve. However, the challenges all seem to be mental, since physically I have an abundance of energy. In fact, I have more energy after a few days of fasting than I have after eating a heavy meal.

If you choose to do a one-day fast, use it as an opportunity to reprogram your RAS. Empower the day by giving it special meaning. Allow the fast to be a metaphor for a meaningful goal, such as optimal health or a better relationship with your spouse. As you visualize your body eliminating everything that would interfere with your goal, you also see your body systems and cells all working together in harmony.

My fasting days are days of heightened awareness. I feel as if I am part of a beautiful poem. Flowers appear to be particularly dazzling, the air seems more fragrant, the birds sound sweeter, and stress-releasing insights occur more frequently. When I do longer fasts, an interesting dialogue often occurs in the morning between my ego and my more aware self. Ego tries to persuade me to stop the fasting. My more aware self has to remember not to argue with ego, because that is ego's realm and ego has an answer for everything. My more aware self invites ego to tell me more.

For me, fasting is an opportunity to pay attention and learn more about the ways that my ego limits my performance and very experience of life.

Had you told me once that I would ever fast for forty days, I'd have reacted with hysterical laughter. The thought would have been so far out from my reality that it could only seem ludicrous. After years of fasting, however, my health is improved and the aging process seems to have slowed down considerably. Fasting is not drudgery and has been both fun and satisfying.

EXERCISE

I am not trying to provide a "how to" guide for fasting; rather, I want to introduce you to the concept. Fasts of more than two days require you to break your fast in certain ways and require additional guidelines. However, you can create one solitary fasting day for yourself just to see how easy it is and how much fun it can be. Your self-esteem will rise and you'll feel a sense of accomplishment. If it is the first time that you have spent a day fasting, make it special by beginning the day with a ritual. Empower your fast by stating your intentions or internalizing affirmations that will serve your growth.

If you feel empowered and more clear after your fast, you may wish to do another fast for a longer period of time. Or perhaps you might consider adding one fast day per week to your usual routine. As always, talk to your health-care professional for specific fasting guidelines regarding hydration and your specific health issues. There are many things you need to be aware of when undertaking a fast, and I am not going to go through all of them here in our limited discussion of the topic. However, if you are seriously thinking of adding fasting to your spiritual practice, read as much as you can on the subject. One point I have never seen in print but have learned from experience is the importance of ingesting electrolytes during longer fasts. These are easily provided by commercial sports drinks that advertise on the label they contain electrolytes. Without these added electrolytes, fasting can cause uncomfortable muscle cramps.

14
Head Shaving
Taking Charge of Change

Our deepest fears are like dragons
guarding our deepest treasure.
–Rainer Maria Rilke

I've always been surprised that whenever I include head shaving in one of my leadership seminars, three times as many women elect to do this than men. Perhaps men harbor a sense of foreboding of the day when they actually have no choice in the matter, whereas women may never get to see their heads naked unless they elect to shave them.

To many, head shaving can be more challenging than jumping out of an airplane. Often, ego fears change more than death. We become so accustomed to relating to the face in our mirror, we eventually identify ourselves as actually being those reflected images, and only that! When the ego identifies you by narrow parameters such as appearance or hair-style, and you start believing that is who you really are, it's a good time to shave your head.

Before the shaving commences, each person who participates tells the group his or her reason for choosing to do it. Reasons vary. One woman said that shaving her head was meant to challenge both her and her friends to see who Linda really was. A man said he felt it aligned him with a long spiritual tradition. Another man said he wanted to shave his head because he was finally willing to see himself as he really was, complete with all the scars on his scalp from his hair transplant. One woman told the group she had always wanted to do it and this was a convenient opportunity.

More than any other reason, people shave their heads to help themselves separate who they really are from who people think they are. It's a matter of seeing the ego and the personality for what they are: distractions that prevent us and others from relating to the real person.

A number of people who have shaved their heads in my seminars call weeks later. They report that their relationships have become more meaningful and that people who they only casually knew before have initiated deep conversations and have broached meaningful and personal subjects.

We are so accustomed to conformity, when we see a nonconformist, the person immediately stands out. Some nonconformists have green, spiked hairdos, strange clothes, numerous facial piercings, or tattoos. Most of us are not inclined to approach someone like that. However, when a person's head is shaved and they exude a serene presence, many people associate this with spirituality and are drawn toward the person. Especially if it is a woman who has shaved her head.

If you do shave your head and are approached by those curious to discuss your motives, use the opportunity to share insights that can help other people grow in their own lives. Don't trivialize the opportunity you have to make a meaningful difference.

LOOK AT YOUR DISCOMFORT

The only thing constant is the certainty of change. Usually, changes are unexpectedly thrust upon us, and then we are left to cope with whatever resources we have on hand. Caught! Totally unprepared. Sometimes, it's nice to take charge of the changes in your life and create specific intentions about what kinds of experiences you want to have as a result of the changes you yourself have orchestrated.

Most people dislike change. They would say that change is bad. It is important for you to see how your RAS is programmed in this area. If it is programmed to label change as bad, reprogram it immediately to label change as good. Change can broaden your horizons by freeing you from the familiar patterns that have controlled your experience of life up until now. If you have become stifled by comfortableness, affirm that change can help you grow, change can show you more of yourself and who you can be.

As with all other extreme approaches to spirituality, you many never actually shave your head. But notice how even reading about it can make your ego uncomfortable. What is it telling you?

Let the idea of head shaving help you examine how you create your reality and how you perceive yourself.

If your RAS has change programmed as bad, you will resist change, and, in the process of resisting, it will harm you. Many people refused to leave their familiar homes when the Nazis invaded, and they lost their lives. By welcoming change, you are empowered to extract every possible atom of positivity from whatever situation arises. All your resources are prepared for peak performance and you will see things with a clearer and more resourceful perspective.

BARING YOURSELF

Before I first shaved my head I was a rather superficial person with a definite image of who he was. Unfortunately, I identified my personality with all my superficial traits. As you may know, the gene for baldness comes from your mother's father. Since my grandpa was bald, I lived with the anxiety that someday my hair might fall out and I would lose what I perceived as my good looks. After I shaved my head I experienced something profound, so radical I had to do a weeklong fast of words so I could be internal with the thoughts the process stimulated. In the end, I was a changed man. I realized that real beauty comes from within. A beautiful person is not necessarily the one with features found on Hollywood actors or magazine models. A person's outward appearance becomes irrelevant when the beauty of their spirit shines forth. Outward appearances change with time, but inner beauty is eternal.

While some of the other extreme challenges seemed to enhance my ego and give it the kind of strength that comes from conquest and victory, this challenge humbled me.

Humility is a natural by-product of ego reduction. When our egos and personalities are set aside, even briefly, by choice or otherwise, we are able to experience a spiritual reality. This spiritual awareness recognizes what is real and what is not real. We are reborn with new eyes. We see all that's associated with ego and personality as just fleeting aspects of who we really are.

The result is an appreciation for the enduring parts of ourselves, like awareness and love. By identifying with our changeless nature, our personalities no longer seem so seductive and we are comfortable with, even nurtured by, just knowing the simple truth of existence. The inner peace that accompanies this depth of knowingness is the essence of extreme spirituality.

EXERCISE

Just do it.

15
Washing Feet
Humility as a Way of Life

*When true simplicity is gained, to bow and to
bend we will not be ashamed.*
–Shaker song

Generally speaking, humility is a virtue. It usually indicates some degree of ego reduction. Of course, the nefarious ego can even flaunt humility to its own ends. This is humorously depicted by a tale of dueling holy men, each trying to be more humble than the other.

> *The first one knelt and said to the other, "I am not worthy to touch your feet."*
>
> *The second replied, "I would be honored to touch the dirt you just walked upon."*
>
> *The dialogue escalated: "I am not even equal to the lint in your navel."*
>
> *"I am but a worm in your excrement."*
>
> *Each man exalted at making himself appear more humble than the other.*

Foolish pride and ego glorification are pretty much universally recognized as the opposite of spirituality. A certain scripture cautions against making public displays of righteousness. An effective way to cultivate your spirituality and lessen your ego is to put yourself into the service of another. But guard against self-aggrandizement. Pay attention and make sure that when you say your intention is to serve another, you are not really intending to build up your own ego.

This is a time in history when good people must step forward and be willing to take responsibility for ensuring our children's future. To paraphrase Edmund Burke: All evil needs in order to flourish is for good people to do nothing. By serving your brothers and sisters, you are serving the whole planet. If people were more concerned with what they were contributing, rather than with what they were getting, we would have heaven on Earth here and now.

Over 80 percent of the world's resources are consumed by 20 percent of the people. There is no shortage of food; that is not the reason for hunger. The reason for hunger is that resources aren't shared proportionately. If there is a shortage of anything at all on the planet, it is a shortage of consciousness and compassion.

In truth, when we selflessly serve another, we in fact are serving ourselves, enhancing our own spiritual and emotional maturity. Whenever we do anything at all that reduces the control our ego has over controlling our realities, we get another glimpse of God. There are so many creative ways to experience this. You could read to a blind neighbor, take an elderly friend grocery shopping, play card games with nursing home residents, pick litter off the shoulder of the road. If you can't think of a way to serve, just pray: Use me, God. Inevitably, those kinds of prayers get answered. Extreme spirituality expresses itself through true selfless service.

A BIBLICAL RITUAL

When Jesus washed his disciples' feet, he was helping them realize that there is no difference between the teacher and the student, no difference between the master and the servant, no difference between the rich and the poor, no difference between the giver and the receiver. Extreme spirituality recognizes God in everyone, including ourselves. From a different tradition comes Neem Karoli Baba, the Indian saint, who said, "Love everyone, serve everyone, and remember God."

In my seminars, I encourage service with a simple foot-washing ceremony. The room is arranged into groups of circles of ten chairs each. One person sits in a chair and another kneels in front of him or her. On the floor in the middle of each circle is a basin of warm water filled with washcloths. Those in the chairs are asked to remove their shoes and socks and place their feet on a folded towel that had been earlier placed before each chair.

Classical music plays while the person on the floor says to the person in the chair, "Please serve me by allowing me to serve you." They then take a washcloth from the basin of warm water, and wash and then kiss both feet. Afterward, both the giver and the receiver spend a moment looking silently into each other's eyes.

The people on the floor continually move to the right until they have washed and kissed the feet of all those seated in the circle. When the circuit has been completed, the people in the chairs change places with those who had been kneeling on the floor, new basins of warm water are brought in, and the exercise is done once again, so that everyone in the seminar has both an experience of giving and one of receiving.

Though it is both beautiful to watch and pleasant to partake in, this simple ceremony is as extreme as smelling a can filled with dog feces, for it is in both these kinds of controlled situations that you have the best opportunities to witness your own ego at work.

Whether we are serving or being served, ego has a response. People seated in the chairs are usually more uncomfortable with this. Even though ego has convinced us that it is generally better to receive than to give, most people discover that their true nature is to feel more comfortable with giving.

LOVE, SERVE, REMEMBER

Before I realized that service is a mandatory part of extreme spirituality, I lived as an island. I did not recycle, I littered, I overconsumed and rarely considered anyone else's needs but my own. After I became more conscious of my role in the universe, I realized that if my liver had cancer, my eye couldn't say, "Not my problem." So it is with social issues. I understood there was a greater reality than the one my RAS had led me to believe was the only reality. I began taking an active part in community service.

If you are a parent, or have a close relationship with someone who is a parent, you know how joyful serving others can be. Parenting is an ideal classroom in which to learn how to put someone else's needs ahead of your own. Though most people would prefer to sleep through the night, new parents will get up many times to feed, nurture, and clean their babies. Even if it seems routine and without much joy, behind it there is a deep satisfaction that is extremely rewarding.

EXERCISE

Recall different occasions when you put someone else's needs ahead of your own. On some of those occasions, you probably felt good about it. On other occasions, you may have indeed put someone else's needs before your own, but you didn't feel totally good about it.

Ask yourself why you don't feel good about some recollections and why you feel fine with others.

You will soon understand it is love that makes the difference. When your heart is open, you feel good about serving others.

16
Loving Your Enemies
Going beyond Forgiveness

Overcome evil with good, falsehood with truth,
hatred with love.
–Peace Pilgrim

Love your enemy? At first, it seemed to me that this was impossible. Then, as I began considering it, just considering the possibility gave me insights into my own residual anger. The cure for anger, I discovered, was compassion. The two are linked like two sides of a coin.

Once, someone slashed my brand-new studded snow tires. Not only were the tires slashed within twenty-four hours of being purchased, they were slashed on Christmas Eve!

Now, if we only love the people who are nice to us, it's easy. Anyone can do that. It is only when we can love the people who abuse us that we get to experience extreme spirituality.

But on that Christmas morning, when I woke up to find four slashed tires, I wasn't thinking about loving my enemies. Since I had just bought them the day before, I started to grow livid. I thought of myself as a just man. My brand of justice included punishing the perpetrator of any offense against me. And so, normally, I would have instantly exploded with upset and anger.

But then, in that moment, in a flash, I realized I was being given an extraordinary opportunity to practice something I had only known intellectually. Rather than feeling sorry for myself, I could feel compassion for the person who did this. What a miserable, angry, unhappy person this had to be. I would definitely want to be me, and not this other person with feelings that result in destructive behavior. Being the victim in this scenario seemed to me to be the less painful position. You may know someone whose story is so devastating and dramatic that it makes slashed tires seem like small potatoes, but sometimes even life's small injustices can seem to us, as we experience them, the equivalent of a Greek tragedy.

THE BEST GIFT OF ALL

To my astonishment, I found myself with my heart open, thinking compassionately of the perpetrator. I could never have imagined the empowerment. Instead of feeling like a victim is supposed to feel, I felt like a spiritual master. It was a dazzling experience of something that had remained mysterious to me for years: if you are to practice extreme spirituality, at some point, you must begin to actively love your enemies.

Author Mary Crowley is quick to remind us that people need loving the most when they deserve it the least. When you do something as radical as loving your enemies, the RAS almost goes into a convulsion! This kind of response to life goes against almost everyone's programming. We are not programmed to love those who hurt us. It goes against our survival instinct. That is why you find few people practicing this one of

Jesus' directives. Even those who would call themselves dedicated Christians have a hard time with this one. But, as humans, we've evolved past the point where only the fittest, the most able to fight, survive.

Begin to practice forgiveness. Make a list of every person and situation you haven't yet forgiven. Regularly go through the list and see who you are ready to forgive. Do whatever it takes to heal the hurt, whether it is by saying affirmations, writing a letter, or making a phone call. When you feel complete, surround the incident with a mentally constructed pink bubble and watch it float away. Practice forgiveness every day. It takes work, but it is worth the effort.

This cannot be done intellectually. Loving forgiveness takes work. You will always know whether you are practicing forgiveness properly by checking the way you physically feel. If you are feeling anything but ecstasy, you are in your head and not your heart.

After you've mastered forgiveness, you can take the exercise to the next level, which is to actually love those who abuse you. Understandably, this can be difficult; yet, until you are able to do this for the first time, you will never understand what the result can be. This aspect of extreme spirituality is not unlike firewalking, skydiving, or breaking a brick. And the results are no less awesome.

When you struggle with forgiveness and loving someone who has hurt you, ask yourself, "Is this worth closing my heart for?" In the words of Sosigenes:

> *The anger of a good man lasts but a moment, no matter what the provocation. The anger of a superficial man lasts two hours. The anger of a heartless man will last a day and a half. For the truly evil man, anger lasts a lifetime.*

EXERCISE

Make a mental list of all the people you know and rank them in order, starting with those you like most and ending with those you like least.

Who is at the very bottom of the list? Probably someone you detest. Perhaps your Uncle Slimy?

Now imagine this scenario: You have reserved a mountain cabin for yourself. You want to spend a few days in seclusion, and you take with you your favorite books, foods, and music. Shortly after you settle into your cabin, an unexpected blizzard strikes. However, you are well prepared, and you are actually pleased to be so insulated and alone with your favorite things in this snowbound cabin.

All of a sudden, in through the door stumbles Uncle Slimy.

As you do this exercise, hold a mental picture of Uncle Slimy in your mind's eye. How does that image make you feel? Imagine being cooped up with him for several days in a snowbound cabin. How does that make you feel?

As a student of extreme spirituality, you now know that it is not Uncle Slimy creating the negative feelings you are experiencing, it is *you* yourself creating them by your reactions to Uncle Slimy. The crux of this exercise is for you to be able to love your Uncle Slimy unconditionally.

Close your eyes and speak to your uncle. Say out loud, I am going to spend these few days in this cabin with you, and here is how I am going to keep my heart open. . . .

You may not actually be able to open your heart at this point in time. Yet, by doing the exercise, you may at least learn intellectually what you will have to eventually do if you want to reap the power that comes from loving those who are usually classified as unlovable.

17
Active Suffering
Accepting the Unacceptable

You can have peace if you find meaning in your suffering.
—Viktor Frankl

A young mother is said to have proudly paraded her newborn among the neighbors saying, "Look at this little Buddha. He is living in bliss." After admiring the beautiful baby, one of her neighbors gently corrected her, "A Buddha is one who has gone beyond suffering and then attains bliss. The baby hasn't suffered enough yet to be a Buddha."

Emotional suffering is the fruit of negative emotions, not negative experiences. What do I mean by suffering? Suffering is hate, anger, fear, pain, defensiveness, resentment, anxiety, jealousy, insecurity, depression, or grief about someone or some incident.

The truth, plain and simple, is that if you are still suffering, then you have not suffered enough. The suffering is not the result of an incident; it is the reaction to the incident. I am not saying you need traumatic incidents, but unless you learn a spiritual response to these kinds of incidents, it seems they keep recurring until you learn the lessons they were meant to impart. This is a profound spiritual truth.

Human suffering can be purposeful. It is like the heat inside an oven. Even when all the right ingredients have been combined, we still need to be cooked as a necessary part of growth. Our suffering helps us grow into the persons we become. I have learned to say "thank you" for my suffering.

If you're still in the cooker experiencing the heat, it's perfectly OK. As long as you are suffering, you can be assured that you haven't suffered enough. You will be fully cooked when you consciously decide not to suffer any more. When you have learned whatever you need to know from suffering, then you can decide to get your lessons through positive experiences instead. Only you and you alone have the power to end negativity in your life. It is called personal responsibility.

YOU AREN'T A VICTIM

So long as you blame someone or something for your suffering, you will feel like a helpless victim, waiting for someone or something outside yourself to rescue you. That just keeps you in the cooker.

An open heart feels a lot better than a closed heart. Positive feelings are far more enjoyable than negative feelings. However, it isn't simply a matter of choosing to open your heart once to end suffering. You must remain conscious and choose again and again and *again* to open your heart and to keep it open if you are to end your suffering and if you are to avoid slipping back into your old patterns.

The best way to be liberated from the constricting programming of the RAS is to go into your suffering actively so that you can see how your RAS produces exactly what you say you don't want. For example, when you really get into your anger, you will discover that you are not really angry about what you thought was making you angry. Our negativity is often linked to things we've never looked at before. A lot of confusion gets resolved simply by embracing, rather than running from, emotional pain.

This active suffering might feel very intense at times, for after all, here you are already in the oven, and now it's being suggested that the heat be turned up even higher.

Specifically, look inside your head and pay attention to what you are telling yourself at the exact moment you are experiencing the greatest pain. Can you imagine saying something else? What could you say that would create a different inner experience? If you are ready to take responsibility for keeping your heart open, you will do or say whatever is needed. First, however, you must reaffirm that you have indeed made the conscious decision to keep your heart open.

WITHOUT PERSISTENT PRACTICE, GOOD CAN TURN BAD

I knew a young man, John, who was kind and considerate. He was a spiritual man. However, as the years progressed, he became a bitter, hateful, and mean individual. What happened?

As happens to many of us when we begin to get older, John had become dissatisfied with his life. Instead of reevaluating himself and how he could change his life, he started to blame others. Once he stopped taking responsibility for his life, he began acting badly and justified his poor behavior with excuses: I was abused, I was cheated, I was deprived . . .

He abandoned the rituals that he used to do to keep himself anchored in a spiritual, growth-centered reality.

JEWELS MUST BE GROUND TILL THEY SPARKLE

John had not suffered enough. His life had been easy, without the friction that generates heat. And since we all need heat, to be cooked at some point, John was past due for some serious suffering.

He will continue to suffer until he has suffered enough. At that point, he can say, "Enough!" and take responsibility for his suffering; he will no longer pretend that he is a victim of circumstances beyond his control. He'll learn that he must look inside himself to see what needs to change. He will see that it is not so much what happens to you, it's what you do about it. It is possible to keep one's heart open, no matter what happens.

NOT TO GROW IS MORE PAINFUL

Unless you understand that suffering is a response, you can never choose a different response. However, after you realize that you are not a pre-programmed robot and have the ability to choose how you are going to react, even with very intense trauma, you can create the same experience as any other person who has ever overcome their suffering through emotional and spiritual growth. You can choose your response. You can choose to learn from and grow with any life circumstance.

Once you decide that you've suffered enough and to take responsibility to end your suffering, everything is a lesson, a game, and can even be an enjoyable exploration. Life may still hand you tough situations, but you will definitely no longer be suffering. Remember, growth can be intense, but the alternative sucks.

If you are still suffering, then obviously you are at that stage of your life where you are *supposed* to be suffering. So at least appreciate that your suffering serves you by providing the fuel needed to move you to the next level. Eventually, you will declare with great gusto, "I have suffered *enough!*" The gusto creates the energy that consciousness growth requires. Suffering can accelerate your growth—or not. You decide what you want from your suffering, and where you want it to take you: forward or backward, or stuck and going nowhere.

Suffering is meant to be a chapter in your life; not the entire story. Albeit the chapter may be very, very, very long, yet the story moves on . . . if you are willing to move on.

EMOTIONAL SUFFERING IS SPIRITUAL SUFFERING

Suffering is always emotional suffering. If we are in physical pain, the suffering is our emotional response to the pain. Suffering is not the pain itself or a necessary by-product of pain. It is a reaction to pain and painful situations, such as the death of a family member. A way to end the suffering, even in the midst of horrific pain, is to see the source of the pain as a challenge, and use it to grow. Extreme spirituality views all emotional and psychological growth as spiritual growth.

I've worked as both a hospital and hospice volunteer. I've witnessed people in monumental pain. Some face it with equanimity and inner peace, while others scream and writhe. Why the different reactions? Some people feel like small kids being punished and the pain is like being whipped with a strap. Others see themselves as so much bigger than the body having the pain that it seems relatively small by comparison. My own insight into suffering came after my car accident. Months had passed and I spent many nights in an agony of pain. One night I cried out, "God, why am I suffering so!?" The answer was instantaneous, "Because that's the only time you turn to *me*." I experienced an amazing tranquility in that moment and was overcome by peace. No God, no peace. Know God, know peace.

If your suffering makes you a wiser, more compassionate and generous person, it has served a good purpose. If your suffering brings you to God, it has served a great purpose.

EXERCISE

If you are suffering right now, remember the story of the monk, the tigers, and the strawberry. Consciously influence your experience of suffering by looking for strawberries and focusing your attention on them instead of the obvious tigers.

Another thing you can do is to reframe the situation so that you can create value with it. Instead of telling yourself that you are weak because you were abused and that's bad, you can tell yourself that you are strong because you were abused and that's good.

Disasters break some people and empower others to greatness. You can be the kind of person that can create a new response to life at any moment you choose. Haven't you suffered enough?

18
Invisible Guidance
Developing an Inner Pendulum

Intuition is soul guidance, appearing naturally in man during those instants when his mind is calm.
–Paramahansa Yogananda

It is comforting and empowering to have help with any formidable task. And believe me, nothing is more formidable than self-transformation. Fortunately, help is always available to you, when you practice extreme spirituality, in the form of invisible guidance, or grace. Let it help you attain your spiritual goals.

I'll describe one technique of how you can put invisible guidance to work for you. Tie a ring or other weighty object to the end of a foot-long piece of string. Congratulations! You've just constructed an organic biofeedback device, commonly known as a pendulum.

By holding the string and letting the ring hang free, you can watch and see what movement occurs in response to yes or no questions. A force within, more subtle than the ego and RAS, causes the pendulum to swing to or fro, north to south or east to west. It can go clockwise or counterclockwise. The pendulum itself is not providing the answers. You are the force that subtly determines the way the pendulum moves.

Once you've determined how the pendulum produces answers for you (for example, a clockwise movement may indicate yes; a back and forth movement indicates no), you can pose questions and watch the pendulum, trusting that the answer is coming from a higher power than your own ego. Ask the question with your rational mind, and then acknowledge the answer as coming from your inner source of invisible guidance.

Your physical body, too, can be an excellent source of guidance. Pay attention to the inner voices that offer you counsel in any particular situation. Notice which is the one voice that creates the most relaxation in your body. Follow that guidance. Listen to the inner voice you're hearing when your back tenses up, when your stomach gets upset. Banish that voice!

Sometimes, when people want guidance in a particular situation, they silently ask themselves, "What would Jesus, or Gandhi, do?" This question is a powerful tool to help you step outside your situation, and your ego, and see objectively. Because these two men are among our greatest examples of humans living with an open heart, simply contemplating their reaction to your situation creates a felt sense of what action would be appropriate using their standards. I have a friend who uses this technique, but substitutes Captain Picard from *Star Trek*, and it still works! Anyone whose life you admire, who lives with compassion, acceptance, and love, can be your guide.

I cherish this aspect of extreme spirituality. It allows for a personal relationship with the unseen universe.

SUPPORT 24/7

Like an internal help hotline, it is comforting to know that your internal support and guides are available twenty-four hours a day, seven days a week. Once you tune into them, you'll learn to recognize your maturing intuition as the force that brings you more of what you want and less of what you don't want.

You can experience receiving love and support from the power that created you, and from which you have never been separated, so that instances of intuition will be recognized as the nurturing and caring God has for you. Beneficent coincidences and fortuitous moments of synchronicity will be seen as signs confirming your spiritual connection and evidence of your extreme spirituality.

IMAGINATION RULES

There are no rules to the relationship you create with your internal guidance. You can fabricate an angel that follows you wherever you go. You can use your angel as a sounding board to discuss ideas and plans, or for support during an exam. You can have an angel who pokes fun at you, helping you see the humor in your ego struggles. You can have as much fun as you want and still receive the spiritual benefits of letting a higher power guide your life.

Don't limit the ways that guidance can come to you. Pray for it. Look for omens. Consult oracles. Seek visions. Visit a psychic. Explore channeling. Talk to nature spirits. Buy a Ouija board. After all, guidance is that quality that connects us *individually* to the Great Spirit.

EXERCISE

Do you ever ask for a sign from above, or from within, to help you make a decision? The answers can be significant and profound, or hilarious. For example, you're at the used-car lot, trying to decide whether to purchase a particular used car. You ask for a sign, and then, within three seconds, a large bird defecates on its windshield. You might reasonably interpret this as an answer to your question!

As an exercise in extreme spirituality, actively seek invisible guidance. Ask for signs, and then look for them. You can also ask for guidance in how to interpret the signs you find. You will, in effect, be forming a relationship with your own inner pendulum that will let you know which signs you can trust and which you can't.

If the notion of guidance appeals to you, you may wish to purchase a copy of the *I Ching*. It has been used as a reliable form of guidance for many thousands of years. It's been perceived as being so accurate that countless Chinese rulers relied on its unerring guidance for centuries.

19
Voluntary Simplicity
Living beneath Your Means

*Freedom's just another word for nothing left to
lose . . . you've got nothing if you ain't free.*
–Kris Kristofferson

The Buddha told us that attachment causes suffering. The more posses-
sions we are attached to, the greater our potential for loss and suffering.
The Bible notes that where your treasure is, that's where your heart will
be. Hindu scriptures urge, again and again: Simplify! Simplify!
Simplify! Though most people grasp this concept intellectually, a pared-
down lifestyle is definitely an extreme practice and very few people actually embrace voluntary simplicity.

Does a simplified lifestyle foster spiritual attainment, or is it spiritual attainment that leads to a simple life? The answers are yes and yes. A
simple life means less time spent acquiring stuff, whatever stuff means to
you. Less time is needed to maintain and protect your stuff and no anxiety is spent on concerns that your stuff might become obsolete or out-
dated. If your stuff isn't demanding all your attention, you can use the
extra time for spiritual growth. Your stuff is often just a big distraction.

Trading an acquisitive lifestyle for spiritual growth may seem like strange behavior to your acquaintances. After all, in our culture, having a lot of stuff is equivalent to having a lot of success. When you embrace simplicity as a practice of extreme spirituality, you sometimes outgrow old friendships.

When we consciously choose to live more lightly as an exercise in extreme spirituality, amazing things can happen. Once we are freed from the busyness that is required to maintain most lifestyles, even lifestyles within our means, we can be liberated from the busyness that goes on within our heads as well. The outer busyness and the inner busyness are just reflections of each other.

If you live in debt, you feel like you are on an endless treadmill; all the energy you might be using for personal growth is being expended by juggling bills. Living beneath your means and having time to work on yourself is a glowing example of extreme spirituality in practice. Instead of buying a brand-new car, for example, you can buy a late-model used car that has low mileage and still runs like new. Instead of dining at expensive restaurants, you can eat out less frequently and occasionally patronize eateries that cost a little less. The transition does not have to be severe; just make little changes here and there and you will be amazed at how much less you're spending.

When you live beneath your means, you always have a surplus and can share generously with others. When you live beneath your means, you feel secure and relaxed. When you live beneath your means, you have the time and energy to do spiritual practices. When you live beneath your means, you help preserve the environment by consuming less of our natural resources.

Because I choose to live a simple lifestyle in a small mountain cabin, I can afford to support charitable causes. I have more time for parenting, community service, reading, hiking, yoga, meditation, appreciating the wildflowers, playing my guitar, sitting by the river, delving into hobbies, and soaking in my hot tub. I can vacation more often and can travel to take courses for my own personal development.

I even present some seminars in my home, precisely because my lifestyle makes a statement. It is a demonstration of what I believe. Let your life be an example to others, also.

'TIS THE GIFT TO BE SIMPLE

An old Shaker song begins, "'Tis the gift to be simple, 'tis the gift to be free." Throughout history, we see extremely spiritual people such as Francis of Assisi, Buddha, Lao Tsu, and others choosing to live in radical simplicity. There is much to be learned from them. Many of these spiritual role models began their lives surrounded by wealth, but later rejected that lifestyle and embraced voluntary simplicity. Even in some poor Third World countries I've visited, where life is simple by necessity, there is a palpable sense that everyday people are living with less stress than we are here in the United States of America. Of course they have stress if they are victims of hunger, disease, corruption, and violence; but in countries like Mexico where people have food and a simple lifestyle, the people living in small villages do not seem unhappy. They have not been conditioned by television advertising that encourages them to be dissatisfied unless they have the latest item being hawked by Madison Avenue PR firms.

The next time you go to a mall, study the people. Instead of enjoying the environment carefully created by the mall designers for shoppers' pleasure, you'll see people rushing around or in a daze, oblivious to the fountains, trees, sculptures, and plants. Instead of playing like kids at a fair, people look weary, stressed, and unhappy.

VOLUNTARY SIMPLICITY IN ACTION

I have a wealthy friend, a very spiritual man. He is considered eccentric by some because he lives in a rented room. He drives an old Dodge. Outwardly, nothing would reveal to a stranger that this man is a multi-millionaire. Voluntary simplicity! What does he do with his time and money? After returning from his law office, he spends time reading and meditating. He invests his money and uses it to fund a foundation he created to help others.

Another friend is almost a billionaire. He lives lavishly. Yet he too is a spiritual man . . . and he too lives far beneath his means. At first appearance, you would never know he is a simple, spiritual man. But the truth is, he has no attachment to the material trappings around him. He is a devout Buddhist. He spends huge amounts of money on good causes and works tirelessly serving and assisting others. His favorite cause is helping children. He has established vocational schools in poor countries so that underprivileged kids can learn skills that will make them employable. One such school teaches children how to cook, and then helps them in getting jobs at fancy hotels.

Before I began simplifying my life, I was a classic worrier. I worried about money and bills. I worried about status, or the lack thereof. I worried about having trivial knickknacks. What do you worry about? Would some of that worry be reduced if you simplified your life voluntarily and were living beneath your means?

EXERCISE

If the notion of living beneath your means appeals to you, create a strategy to attain exactly that. Take an inventory of your lifestyle and note where you can simplify. Sometimes this will prompt you to make many small changes in your life. Perhaps you can attend one less show each month, eat at home more often, purchase clothes that aren't made by an expensive designer. It may, however, prompt you to make some extreme changes, like selling your home and buying a much smaller house; one that is amply comfortable but enables you to live beneath your means. As you set goals that will effect a change in lifestyle, also create goals for personal growth and service, because, finally, you'll have some extra time on your hands.

20
Seeing Yourself as Divine
Discovering God Within

Namaste
(The God in me salutes the God in you)
—Hindu salutation

When you become adept at experiencing life without your RAS limiting your perceptions, and when you are not being continually distracted by the activities of your ego, the true nature of things appears to you. Your clarity gives you a direct experience of God. You realize that the God you've always sought is simply the awareness that sees the sunset through your eyes and hears the birds sing through your ears. This conscious awareness is the Godhead as you. Meditation is meant to give you this experience.

My most advanced leadership seminars include an activity to assist people in attaining an insight into their own divinity through the altar process. Participants penetrate the illusion of separation, the false perception of ever being disconnected from that which created them.

THE ALTAR PROCESS

The altar process works like this: Everyone leaves the room and goes outside into nature. People are to bring back berries, branches, flowers, crystals, anything they wish to contribute to the construction of a large altar. In addition to the items gathered from outside, I add fruit, statues, incense, and holy pictures.

My assistants collect what people gather and assemble the altar while participants are still outside the seminar room. The altar always looks beautiful. In fact, I'm constantly amazed that such incredible beauty can be created within an impromptu exercise. What cannot be seen by the group, when they return after a recess, is that out of sight behind the altar is a huge mirror.

Relaxing music is played, chants are started, and one by one, each person is silently led to the altar and seated on it, in a special place made for that purpose. The group is instructed to focus all their love, adoration, and passion for God onto the person sitting upon the altar. People are to worship that which lies *within* the person enthroned on the altar.

The person on the altar now sees the mirror for the first time. And what they see is their own reflection, surrounded by flowers, incense, and fruit. They see themselves being worshipped by a roomful of open-hearted, loving people. Ultimately, they see something within themselves—the divinity in them that is God incarnate. It is the process of God remembering that He or She chose to forget about being God in order to experience what it's like to be an individual man or an individual woman. And in the remembering, there is a sense of reunion or "coming home."

SEEING YOUR TRUE SELF

In the moment the person on the altar penetrates the illusion that they are separate from our creator, they experience the oneness of the dreamer and the dream. They realize that there is no separation between the creator and the creation. You can choose to either *be* the dreamer or be *in* the dream, just as God can choose to be divine or to be incarnate, as a human. As you, the dreamer, look through the eyes of each character in one of your dreams, you are able to experience something through each of them. This is the same way that God is experiencing your life *through* you.

Sitting upon the altar, people frequently are able to surrender, for the very first time, to this new reality wherein they know themselves to be the divine in human form. When this dawns on many of them, it looks like astonishment, joy, and tears all in an instant. Frequently, they burst into laughter. It is both emotionally overwhelming and enlightening. Yet, people usually experience a sense of "Aha," rather than "Wow!!!"

Before you realize that it is God who resides inside you and is expressing through you, you might feel extremely insecure. Yet, after you realize the true nature of God, and you feel the empowerment that comes with this insight, you also see that God is in everyone else as well. No one isn't God.

When you discover and rejoice in your own divinity, you are better able to understand more people and to love them and serve them as well. When you feel separate and insecure, you keep your distance. Once you know you have God *within* you, all things are possible.

EXERCISE

You will need a partner for this exercise. Select someone you feel comfortable with and sit at a small table in a darkened room with a candle burning between you. The dark room and flickering candlelight will create a mood of shadowy, safe intimacy.

Gaze into each other's left eye. Allow your gaze to soften its focus so that your partner's face at times seems blurred. Just notice that your eyes will start going in and out of focus on their own. As they do, your partner's face will seem to morph as the candle flickers and your own eyes lose and regain their focus.

Let your partner's face change. Don't try to refocus your eyes. You will see that at times your partner looks like someone completely different. At other times he or she will seem incredibly old or impossibly young. Sometimes he will seem beautiful and sometimes ugly. The transfigurations before you may make you laugh. Just keep maintaining eye contact with your partner's left eye.

Hopefully, at a certain point, you will feel a connection to the spirit peering out at you from within your partner's left eye. You will observe that, although his outer form seems to change, you have connected with something changeless. Also, since your partner is doing the same exercise along with you, he or she has connected with something changeless in you.

This changeless spark is the spirit that resides in every living person. It is the God within.

21
Embracing the Spiritual Perspective
The Universe Is Perfect

A bell is not a bell until you ring it.
A song is not a song until you sing it.
And the love that is in you wasn't put there to stay;
Love isn't love until you give it away.
—Anonymous

EVERYTHING IS PERFECT

When I do group spiritual counseling, my objective is simple: all that needs to happen is for people to shift paradigms. Instead of living in a paradigm that includes judgment, insecurity, and a host of other negative emotions, you can make a conscious decision to live in a paradigm where the spiritual perspective is the undisputed solution to every problem. In this way, you see things from God's point of view, and at some level, everything must ultimately be seen as perfect.

Some situations are more difficult than others when trying to see perfection. For example, you may not at first find anything perfect about a nuclear bomb. Yet it is precisely the horror of the atomic bomb that brought many people into the peace movement. The bomb stimulated consciousness growth on a mass scale.

Even war at some level must be seen as perfect. The tormented and the tormentors must be seen in a way that is greater than a single lifetime. By perceiving a spirit as spanning lifetime after lifetime, as many cultures that believe in reincarnation do, we can assume that—over time—we are all going to collect the exact experiences that are needed. Because the universe *is* perfect.

The dynamic of the group is a process where people share their situations and everyone else assists them in finding and embracing a spiritual perspective. Like anything else worth attaining, it takes commitment, time, and practice. But extreme spirituality is worth the effort.

CHOOSING APPROPRIATE RESPONSES

The spiritual perspective includes the knowledge that everything is God, without exception. Knowing that the universe is perfect, you realize that you, plus all the circumstances of your life, are perfect. When you embrace the spiritual perspective, you strive for change while you continue to grow. You oppose evil, because you aim for excellence. But at the same time that you oppose a Hitler or a Milosevic or a Stalin, you feel compassion for who they are, and you understand the cause of their evil. The universe, in its perfection, allows for the blackest of the black, the whitest of the white, and everything in between. In each lifetime, you can choose which it will be for you.

Many mystics say that it is a matter of being *in* the world, but not *of* it. You perceive life as a metaphysical game. You are totally involved, but totally detached, residing in that place behind the RAS where you can simply be a witness.

What you do does not necessarily look any different before and after you shift paradigms. What has changed is where you are coming from when you do it.

LESSONS OF THE SAMURAI

Samurai warriors did not kill and slaughter because they were bloodthirsty. On the contrary, they killed and slaughtered as a spiritual exercise in serving their leaders without question. Extreme spirituality, as you've seen, is sometimes quite a messy affair. The fierce samurai were killing machines by day; yet at night, they wrote poems and wept as comrades shared poetry by the campfire.

The samurai were trained to always behave with honor. If a samurai lived and died with honor, he was assured that he would be reincarnated again as a samurai. So there was no feeling of loss in death. But if a samurai did not live and die with honor, he would receive the most horrible consequence: to be reincarnated as something other than a samurai.

One samurai witnessed his master being killed. Since the code of the samurai required him to avenge his master's death, he spent months tracking the assailant. Finally, he cornered the killer in a blind alley. As he drew his sword to behead the cornered man, the killer spat in the samurai's face.

With that, the samurai slowly and calmly put his sword back into its sheath, turned, and started to walk away.

The bewildered man called after him, "Why didn't you kill me?"

The samurai answered, "Because you angered me."

A samurai was trained to never kill with anger, but from a sense of duty. It was a matter of honor. To kill with anger would mean that you acted dishonorably, and you would be destined to lose your samurai spirit when you died. This was not only a personal disgrace, it was also seen as disgracing your teachers and your master.

Samurai warriors knew that an act, in and of itself, was no indication of honor. It was the state of the samurai's mind that determined honor.

The lesson of the samurai teaches us that it is not what we do per se that is important, but rather where our consciousness is while we are doing whatever it is that we do. For example, you can repair a broken pipe in your garden while muttering curses and growling with frustration, or you can perform the same act while humming a joyous hymn.

DETACHING BEFORE REACTING

When you can remain detached from what you are doing, you see life more like a movie.

Instead of being a character in the movie, however, you now have the choice of stepping from the movie into the audience. The key here, of course, is the word "choice." Most people do not have a choice as to how they will react and behave in certain situations. Most people are trapped inside the movie and are very robotlike. If you were to push certain of their buttons, it would be possible to know exactly how they would respond: totally predictable. They have no choice. They cannot "step back" and be detached.

By seeing the spiritual perspective, you *are* extreme spirituality in action. You are liberated from automatic and predictable responses. You are free. This freedom is an internal state; it is the peace that surpasses all understanding. Because you are no longer reactive, you are able to consciously create your own reality.

BEST POSSIBLE SOLUTION

Before deciding to live in a paradigm where the spiritual perspective is the only solution to every problem, you will constantly try solutions that—within themselves—always seem to have the seeds for more problems. After you realize that embracing a spiritual perspective always provides the best possible solution, your heart will stay open to people and circumstances that used to shut you down. Your RAS will relax its grip on you and you will enjoy more comfort and ease, regardless of where you are, who you're with, or what's happening.

FOR GOD'S SAKE, BE HAPPY!

Within you is the God-given capacity to experience real joy and happiness. But do you live in a state of joy?

There can be no higher experience than the joy that comes from inner peace, love, and spiritual clarity. Rather than perceiving your own happiness as indulgent, realize that there is no greater gift that you can give the world than moments wherein you experience your bliss. It is also a gift back to your creator. If you are happy, God is happy. Just as God appreciates the sunset through your eyes, God experiences happiness and joy by creating you as a receptor through which to have the experience.

IT'S ABOUT TIME

This book's purpose is to motivate you to consciously create the reality you want. On your spiritual journey, you may employ some of the ideas expressed here, or you might seek something more traditional. Or you may blaze your own trail.

The means you use to become more conscious are not as important as are your efforts to create a joy-filled reality. Regardless of your path, every human's ultimate goal should be to create more love, joy, and happiness, not only for ourselves, but for everyone else as well.

You create your own reality! Are you getting it? You create your reality with your beliefs. Whatever you believe about life ultimately becomes your experience of life. If you believe in miracles, you can experience miracles. If you do not believe in miracles, you can never experience them. Pay attention to your beliefs.

You create your own reality.

Be happy!

EXERCISE

The next time you notice yourself disturbed by something, immediately enlarge your perspective on the situation until you can see that it is perfect just the way it is, and that you can use the opportunity for growth.

For example, most parents try to spare their children any discomfort. Yet by trying to make our children's lives easy, we can deprive them of the ability to learn from trial and error. Therefore, at one level it seems like your kids are making mistakes, but a spiritual perspective helps you see that the mistakes are actually opportunities to learn and to grow. Practice restraining yourself from immediately getting involved in a child's dilemma, even though your first impulse is to jump right in and save the child from failure. See perfection in the situation by assuming a spiritual perspective.

To achieve an objective perspective, you might have to back away from the incident sooooo far that it seems you are witnessing it from outer space.

When you back far enough away, you see clearly that the universe is always perfect.

APPENDIX
Tolly's Theory of Firewalking
(Reprinted from www.firewalking.com)

OVER TWO MILLION WESTERNERS HAVE FIREWALKED.

Knowing the secret behind firewalking can improve your life! Even if you never do it yourself, knowing how it works can bring you better health and increased personal power. Why? Because firewalking demonstrates how your thoughts impact everything else in your life. Thoughts change brain chemistry, and that results in an alteration of body chemistry as well. This is immediately apparent when you entertain a sexual fantasy. Firewalkers are instructed to pay close attention to their thoughts, since those very thoughts are the way in which we create our own realities. Positive thinkers literally live in a different chemical environment than negative thinkers. They impose less stress on their immune systems, and the result of that should be obvious.

I have been researching firewalking since 1977 and am considered to be the foremost authority on the subject. Because of this work, the United States now has the largest firewalking culture in history. Never before have so many people participated in this ancient ritual which had previously been reserved for only a select few. My ideas regarding the phenomenon have evolved over time and now I feel enough confidence in my point of view to publish my own theory about why people are not burned when walking on glowing, red coals. My theory is remarkably different from all the others, but I have found each of the other theories flawed in one way or another.

WATER VAPOR THEORY DISMISSED

One theory I encountered on the subject was based on the "Leidenfrost Effect." Several physicists suggested that the moisture on the sole of the foot created a vapor barrier that prevented the foot from actually contacting the coals. The analogy was proposed that firewalking is similar to licking your finger and touching a hot iron to test whether or not it is up to a sufficient temperature to press a garment. When the iron is hot enough, it literally vaporizes the moisture on a fingertip, and the finger itself is repelled from the iron by water turning to vapor. This is termed the Leidenfrost Effect, named after the man who first described it.

The Leidenfrost Effect can also be easily observed by putting a few drops of water on a hot griddle. When the metal griddle is hot enough, the water beads up and dances around because the heat is so intense that the bottom of the water drop is vaporized before the drop reaches the heated surface and the rising water vapor pushes up against the underside of the drop, causing it to bounce off the escaping steam before it ever reaches the metal.

A physicist by the name of Jearl Walker was so convinced in the validity of this theory that he actually believed it was impossible to get burned while firewalking. After severely injuring himself on a coal bed, he lost faith in this theory. Once, during my early days of research, I observed someone getting burned during a firewalk, and back in the 1970s I rejected this theory that had been based on the Leidenfrost Effect.

CONDUCTIVITY NOT AN ISSUE

Another theory physicists have proposed is the "Conductivity Theory." The analogy used to illustrate this idea was that of reaching into an oven to remove a hot cake pan. The air inside the oven is the same temperature as the metal cake pan, yet one can reach an unprotected hand into the oven without injury. However, if you were to grab the pan itself, the result would usually be a burn. The reason for this is that the air is a poor conductor of heat, while the metal pan is a better conductor. Physicists theorized that the coals were poor conductors and that was why a firewalker's foot was not burned in the coal bed, regardless of its temperature.

In 1994, physicist Bernard Leikind visited the Firewalking Institute and tried to dramatically illustrate this concept by strapping two sirloin steaks to his feet and then walking across a bed of coals while The Discovery Channel filmed the event. The steaks seemed to be unaffected by the coal bed. He then placed a metal grill in the coals and, when it was glowing red, he placed the same steaks on the grill and the metal instantly seared the meat. He felt this sufficiently demonstrated that mental state had nothing to do with the phenomenon of firewalking. He emphasized that it would not be possible for humans to walk on the glowing, red grill without injury.

As soon as he said this, a number of people from our staff walked on the grill without harm.

The grill was so red-hot, the weight of people walking on it bent the softened metal and left impressions of the firewalkers' feet on the grill. We keep the grill with its molded footprints as a souvenir to help debunk the conductivity theory.

When a physicist experiments with fire, the objects of observation are usually not living, conscious subjects. Rules of conductivity can be applied in these instances. However, human beings are dynamic, self-regulating organisms. Thus research into firewalking is really outside the physicist's realm of training. People who research the mind and body are more qualified to propose theories on firewalking than scientists who simply deal with static matter.

It has always been my belief that a person's state of mind is the crucial factor when exploring the science of firewalking. Just because a physicist can walk on the coal bed without harm does little to dismiss the idea that mental state is important. His belief in his theory gives him the confidence to walk on the coals. The "confidence" itself is a mental state. I suggested to Dr. Leikind that we blindfold him and lead him in various directions near the coal bed so that he would have no way of preparing himself mentally before actually stepping onto the embers. He refused. He also refused to walk on the metal grill, so I assumed that at some level he too must have realized there was more to the phenomenon than the conductivity of the coals and simple physics.

In fact, after years of insisting that firewalking was rather safe due to the low conductivity of the coals, with temperature being irrelevant, on May 9, 2000, Dr. Leikind finally signed a statement saying, "Any claim that the temperature of the coals is not important...is simply preposterous"; and adding, "it is my opinion that firewalking is an abnormally dangerous or 'ultra-hazardous' activity."

Yet someone in America recently walked on coals measured at 2,200 degrees Fahrenheit without injury! Obviously, physicists still do not fully understand the process.

Typical firewalks that are open to the public involve coal beds ranging between 1,200 and 1,500 degrees Fahrenheit. Dr. Ron Sato, faculty member of the Stanford University Medical School and director of a nearby burn unit, says that human flesh momentarily exposed to 1,200 degree heat should sustain third-degree burns to the epidermis and dermis, charring the entire thickness of skin to a blackened carbon residue. Dr. Sato has treated people who have accidentally stepped on glowing coals and were so badly burned that they required skin grafts. When commenting about people who voluntarily firewalk without injury, Dr. Sato says, "There's no logical explanation."

BOILING WATER IN A PAPER CUP

Two scientific experiments have helped me form my present theory.

One is a simple demonstration used by school teachers. Perhaps you saw it in your own science class when you were a teenager? The teacher fills a paper cup with water and places it over a flame. The water boils and the cup does not burn. The reason for this is that the water can only reach a temperature of 212 degrees Fahrenheit before it turns to steam. Since the water is in constant contact with the paper cup, the paper cannot get any hotter than 212 degrees. However, in order for the cup itself to burn, it must reach a kindling point, which happens to be higher than 212 degrees. The water maintains the temperature of the paper at a constant 212.

The other experiment was conducted by the United States government during the early days of research into space flight. When a spacecraft reenters the atmosphere, friction heats the craft to extremely high temperatures. It had to be determined whether the person at the controls could still function if the interior of the craft became very hot. To simulate this situation, scientists created a heat chamber. Volunteers entered the chamber and the inside temperature was raised. It was discovered that though an egg was cooking within this atmosphere, the human subjects were unharmed. In fact, the measured air temperature within the nose of a subject was actually cooler than the air in the chamber itself.

MIND IN MATTER

These two experiments form the basis of my own theory regarding firewalking. The reason Dr. Leikind's steaks were seared by the glowing metal while human feet were not is simply because the human foot was connected to a living, conscious being who is more than inert matter. The human body has a mechanism to cool itself. Respiration, perspiration and circulation all play a part in this process and all are connected to the brain, which is obviously influenced by the mind. Observe someone sucking on a lemon, or entertain a few sexual fantasies, and you yourself can instantly see how the mind can change the electro-chemical state of the brain and then the central nervous system relays that electro-chemical change to the body systems and cells of your being.

You can have physical experiences when nothing physical is impacting you. This is not "mind over matter," but rather: "mind in matter."

When a firewalker is in the proper state of mind, the blood flowing through his or her body is akin to the water in the paper cup. The blood is 98.6 degrees Fahrenheit. As it moves through the soles of the feet, it continually cools the tissue and prevents it from reaching its "kindling point," in the same way that the water maintained the temperature of the paper at 212.

Of course there are limits, and it has never been our intention at the Firewalking Institute of Research and Education to push the limits. Rather, we have simply looked for an explanation of the basic phenomenon of firewalking as it has been practiced throughout thousands of years and have sought new applications that can enhance the lives of those of us living in society today.

When humans walk on coals measured at 2,200 degrees Fahrenheit without harm, they are able to do so because the body is obviously capable of cooling and protecting itself up to a certain point. By the way, engine blocks for cars are made by pouring molten metal at 1,100 degrees!

My explanation of why people can walk on glowing coals without injury also implies why some people have in fact been burned. During the 1970s I set out to demystify firewalking and created the world's first firewalking seminar. I trained hundreds of instructors to conduct the seminar around the planet and, as of the year 2000, well over two million people have participated in the firewalking seminar. How many were burned? About 50. Since people are sometimes injured, that too needs to be addressed. (I'm not counting those who've tried to stand still or linger on the coals.)

Injuries underscore that the mind, rather than the coal bed, represents the variable. When people are not in the state of mind that allows all body systems to operate at peak performance, the capillaries constrict and prevent the blood from moving freely through the tissue on the soles of the feet. When that occurs, the blood cannot carry heat away from the sole and cannot maintain the temperature required to prevent burning. The result can be blistering or charring of the skin. Aloe Vera has certain properties that can physically restore this circulation and, when applied immediately after a burn is sustained, blistering can frequently be prevented.

Dr. Andrew Weil, the renowned Harvard-trained physician and medical researcher, has investigated firewalking for many years and says,

"There is no way I can be convinced that mental state is not the key variable in firewalking."

When the subject of conductivity comes up, I think of the times when I have patted the coals with a shovel to even out the embers. The shovel is metal and extremely conductive. As soon as the hot shovel is placed in a bucket of water, it creates an audible "hiss." The shovel is not in the coals any longer than our feet. So the coals obviously conduct the temperature just fine. It seems silly to consider the "conductivity" of a heat source; rather, the issue is about the conductivity of anything placed in contact with the heat source. The metal, being dense, conducts the heat from the source extremely well. Human flesh, however, is not very conductive.

When people burn, it may indicate that their states of mind have made them more "dense." A "fluid" mind-state translates into fluidity of the body itself. So what needs to be examined is not the conductivity of the coals, but why human flesh is sometimes more conductive than at other times.

Because of my extensive research, I now counsel prospective firewalkers to avoid walking on the embers until they take a moment to look inside themselves at all the conflicting inner voices. Some voices will be saying *"Don't walk"* and others will be saying *"Walk!"* I tell people to first listen to each inner voice, then pay attention to the state of your body. Which decision makes your body more comfortable? If the decision to walk makes you feel more comfortable than the decision not to walk, then walk. Because if you are relaxed with your decision, you are in a certain bio-chemical state. Whether the relaxation with the decision to walk is based on a belief in physics or a belief in a higher power, it matters not. Both beliefs create the exact same physiology in the body. Unless their bodies are comfortable with the decision to cross the coals, I suggest people wait for another time.

The body itself is an excellent reflection of mental state. If the body is tense, that is an indication of thought processes that will interfere with the physical mechanisms employed by the body to protect itself. When I say that you must be "relaxed," I do not mean the same kind of relaxed feeling you have when lounging in a hammock. I believe that people who ultimately cross the coals unharmed have a deep sense of knowing that they won't burn their feet—before they even take the first step. Obviously, if you think you're going to get hurt, then you should not step into the coals. You aren't stupid.

After people tell themselves "*I can do this and not get burned*," and they feel "comfortable" with that certainty, they proceed to walk with "confidence." All these states—relaxed, comfortable, confident—indicate a certain chemical condition within the brain and body. Thus, firewalking becomes an exercise in examining the mind/body connection. This is why firewalking is so popular today among athletes, executives and healthcare providers. Anyone seeking to explore the mind/body connection and ways to apply this information toward enhancing human potential will find value in firewalking.

New firewalkers are amazed at the discovery that they themselves are such incredible beings. Firewalking reveals that being a mere human is nothing mere. Our minds are the new frontier and firewalking is just the beginning in the process of self-discovery. The implications of "mind in matter" are truly exciting and can offer new hope to people with severe illnesses as well as anyone seeking to overcome limitations imposed by old beliefs: salesmen, students, athletes—the list goes on and on. It may even include you!

KEYNOTE TALKS AND SEMINARS BY TOLLY BURKAN

If you would like more information about Tolly's seminars, audiotapes or videotapes, you can write to Tolly Burkan & Associates, Box 584, Twain Harte, California 95383-0584. You can also go to www.firewalking.com or www.tollyburkan.com on the Internet. By phone, you can call 800.218.0055 toll-free from anywhere in the United States. From foreign countries, please call 209.928.1100.